My Heart Hurts

a theology of pain and suffering

Andrew Damazio

PUBLISHED BY
Andrew Damazio
Happy Valley, Oregon 97086

My heart hurts: the theology of pain and suffering

9798317357412

CONTENTS

Preface to the Book v
introduction ix
Pick Up the Pieces xxi

PART 1
A THEOLOGY OF SCARS

Where are You 1
When God Let You Down 15
A Better Theology 25
Blinding Pain 35
Wrestling with God 49

PART 2
A GARDEN CALLED GETHSEMANE

Emotional Gethsemane 67
A God Who Bleeds 79
King Jesus 87
Relational Wisdom 95
Jesus Shows Us How To Be Human 121
Navigating Disappointment 163
Conclusion: So Why Does God Allow Pain
and Suffering? 177

PREFACE TO THE BOOK

This is my raw, unfiltered journey through the valley of the shadow of death and back. These words you are about to read are not theory or some fictional story, this book is written by someone who has lived through enough tragedy, loss, and pain, to last for several lifetimes.

These pages mean a great deal to me, because they are flowing from my heart not just my head; they are coming from my life, not stories I have heard.

I wrote "My Heart Hurts" for people who have experienced dark seasons of pain and suffering. Seasons that you thought would never end and you would never get out of. The type of pain so deep that words cannot seem to express the depth. Suffering that shakes the foundations of your soul and makes you question yourself, your friends, and even God himself. These are terrifying waves to weather. I know because I've been there and have lived to tell about it, or in this case, write about it.

My deepest prayer while you read this book is that a glimpse of hope is awakened, that healing begins, and a deep breath of air fills your lungs, for maybe the first time in a while.

For anyone who has ever put their face in their pillow and screamed 'Why?'

For anyone who has wept for so long they lost their voice and all their tears.

For anyone who has tried to help their best friend walk through pain but didn't know what to say.

For anyone who has questioned God and his goodness.

For anyone who has been hurt by the church because your pain got dismissed and you got told to just try harder, to pray harder.

This book is for you.

This is your invitation to come walk with me, cry with me, even argue with me, through a theology of pain and suffering.

I am going to be attempting to give an answer to the question that humans have been wrestling with for millennia, “Why does pain and suffering happen?” and furthermore, “Why does God allow it?”

My only request is this: read the entire book. Don’t skim through pages or skip sections. Please trust that I will answer the question by the end of this book. Every chapter builds upon the one prior, and I know your heart will be stretched and healed as you walk through each page.

Let us begin our journey.

THE INTRODUCTION

The moment I heard the news is seared in my mind forever. Sunday, August 14th 2022 around 4pm. We had just an amazing morning at church. It's summer in the Pacific Northwest, so gorgeous that no one thinks about the 8 months of rain it took to get there. I am at a friend's house having dinner, while the laughter of kids playing in the yard filled the air, life couldn't be better.

My phone buzzes on the table, but I'm mid-meal so I don't pick up and continue chatting. Five seconds later, it buzzes again, and I notice it was one of my older sisters.I have 2 older sisters, Nicole and Bethany, and one younger sister, Jessica.

That's right, no brothers, because God wanted to punish me.

Nicole rarely calls me, we text more than we talk on the phone, and she never calls me multiple times in a row. I took the call and walked outside on the front porch.

"What do you need from me now?" I said sarcastically in a typical younger sibling voice.

Nothing. No response. After a few seconds, I ask, "Hey, you there, can you hear me?"

After another 10 seconds of silence, all I can hear is muffled crying on the other end. Then that feeling came to the middle of my chest just like a movie. The type of feeling where your stomach drops to the floor, your heart skips a bit, and your mind goes to the worst possible scenario, knowing that exact thing happened. I knew something was wrong and I knew what it was.

My sister with shuttering and stammering lips uttered, "She's gone."

I knew who she was talking about and what she was talking about. I didn't need her to explain more than those two words, I just had that sense. My other older sister, Bethany, had died.

All at once, so many emotions, so many questions whirled as my mind raced. The only coherent words that I could get out were "I will meet you at Mom and Dad's" and I hung up. In a daze, I walked back into the house, got my keys, and drove to my parents' house. On the drive I slowly began to feel the adrenaline start to pump through my body as the realization of what had just happened began to set in.

If you have ever experienced something like this, it's a whirlwind; it's very much an out of body experience. You feel numb of emotions yet overwhelmed by them at the same time. Countless words to say without knowing which ones to say. With grieving and processing, so many things start happening at once, it is a multilayered experience. Especially when someone dies, in some ways, it's a very inhumane reality. While you are grieving their death, there are so many things to start doing. Cleaning where they lived, funeral planning, phone calls from the coroner, all of their belongings and where they go, who to tell first and how, the list goes on and on. It's a very disheveling experience, and you do all of this while weeping.

Above all of those thoughts and feelings, I had questions. Questions seemingly no therapist or pastor could answer, only God himself. In the middle of my pain, I began to dive deeply into not just the subject of my faith but the object of my faith. What did I truly believe about God, his word, and his character? This started a silent journey in my heart, deeply wrestling with God, and all the while, my heart grew wearier and wearier.

Let's put a pin in this for just a moment while I give you some back story and then fast forward to a crucial moment in my life, when my inner world came crashing down and my heart broke. I know we're hopping around but stay with me. These pieces all fit together to tell the full story of how this book you are holding right now came to be.

I don't know what kind of upbringing you had, what your parents did for work, but I was raised as a pastor's kid, or also known as a PK. My parents were both pastors, my grandparents on both sides of my family were pastors, and you guessed it—as I write this book I am a lead pastor of a church in downtown Portland. Fits the narrative doesn't it? Though I tried to run from this legacy my entire life until college, I didn't get too far. Pastoring was just something I couldn't shake.

Being raised in church has its benefits and its challenges, for sure. If you were not raised in church, the life of a pastor's kid would take multiple books and a slide show to explain its uniqueness: Being at church 5 days a week. Sleeping in the back pew waiting for the song "I could sing of your love forever" to actually end. Having random people you don't even know spank you —yes I know, that's crazy for a modern reader, but it was the 90's; there were no rules. Being a pastor's kid really marked me, so much so, as a funny but very real representation of my life, I have a tattoo of a fish inside of a fish bowl, and the fish's name is PK.. I have spent my entire life in church, and though it had its challenges, I am actually incredibly grateful for it. It marked me.

Being a PK means you were at church all the time. I mean all the time. Prayer meetings, conferences, retreats, advances, youth group, teaching night, parent night, the list doesn't end. Now being a pastor myself, not much has changed, I am still at church functions all the time.

About a year ago I was at a pastor's conference, not preaching or teaching, just attending and seeing some friends. I was sitting down near the front, of course, as a good PK, and as worship was going on, I sensed the Holy Spirit begin to knock on my heart. I knew he wanted to talk. But I didn't. I just really wasn't in the mood. I was tired, I wanted the service to be over so I could go home and see my wife and 3 kids. But he wouldn't stop knocking. So after about 30 minutes of this, I finally said something like, "can I help you?" After a few seconds I felt the still small voice of the Holy Spirit ask, "So how are you doing?" I responded in a snarky tone, "Great! How are you doing?" I don't know if it's kosher to ask the Holy Spirit how he is doing. Probably the snarkiness isn't, for sure.

A few seconds later, he asked the same question, so I knew he wasn't going to let up. "I'm great," I said, "the church is growing, my wife and kids are the best they have ever been, my friends are the absolute best, Cruz (my oldest son) is doing so well at sports, my heart kinda hurts, but I'm great!" I didn't even know what had slipped out of my mouth. The Holy Spirit said back so gently, "What did you say?" I said it again slowly, a bit more aware of my words this time, “My heart hurts.” It’s the first time I had said it out loud. I kinda knew subconsciously that it was bouncing around in my soul, but I had never given voice to it. And it was the truth: my hurt heart.

The last few years of my life had been intense, and if I had to give one word to sum it all up, it would be Pain. Yes, there had been moments of overwhelming joy in my life: planting Rose Church, having our 3rd child, finding life-long best friends, fun vacations, laughing late into hot summer nights. For sure there were some unbelievably joy-filled moments.

But for the general overview, it has been painful. Difficult. Unfair.

Perhaps you can relate to this kind of poignant duality. On one hand, your life has experienced some joy or success. Meanwhile on the other hand, your life is overflowing with emotional pain, or intense stress, or unbelievable challenges.

For me, even though those wonderful events above had happened, it had also been one of the most painful, unexplainable (words could never do it justice) seasons of my life. To name just a few: my dad got lymphoma cancer, and almost died multiple times. My dad’s best friend and my pastor got ALS out of nowhere, and died. One of my close friends' baby died at 25 weeks. Another friend of mine got incredibly rare stomach cancer at 29 and died. An amazing lady in our church had an oldest son who took his own life, leaving behind his 2 daughters. My best friends went through a horrific season with it ending it divorce. Bethany died at 38 years old tragically. Another one of my close friends' 2 year old daughter got diagnosed with a horrible disease. I was walking through all this while pastoring a new church launch, preaching every Sunday, and trying to stay married and raise 3 young kids.

Pain.

Loss.

Anger.

Confusion.

Sadness.

So many theological questions.

Can you understand why I was standing in that church conference ignoring the gentle knocking of the Holy Spirit? On some level I knew that behind that door was a tsunami of who-knows-what and I had no idea how to not drown. But here I was now, standing in the middle of the aisle during that worship set, losing control. As if I ever had it. My heart hurt. Deeply. And it was the first time I had admitted it and the first time I had said it out-loud.

My friends always make fun of me for being the "I'm fine" guy. That's just my default response. "I'm fine. Life is great." But I wasn't fine. I wasn't good. And the minute I said it, it felt like the dam of my heart broke open and the river of my soul gushed out. For the next several minutes, I word vomited to the Holy Spirit all that I had been through, and when I came to the end, He was silent for maybe 15 seconds. Then a sense of that still, small voice came again, "I know. I have been waiting for you"

I believe Jesus is waiting for many of you as well.

Revelation 3:20 *"Here I am! I stand at the door and knock. If anyone hears my voice and opens the door, I will come in and eat with that person, and they with me"*

He is knocking. He is waiting. For you to open up the door of your heart so that he might come in and commune with you. Eat with you.

I have learned this and probably so have you: life touches us all. No one gets out free of scars.

Tim Keller in his book *walking with God through pain and suffering* writes *"No one is immune. Therefore, no matter what precautions we take, no matter how well we have put together a good life, no matter how hard we have worked to be healthy, wealthy, comfortable with friends and family, and successful with our career—something will inevitably ruin it. No amount of money, power, and planning can prevent bereavement, dire illness, relationship betrayal, financial disaster, or a host of other troubles from entering your life. Human life is fatally fragile and subject to forces beyond our power to manage. Life is tragic."*

This is why we need a theology of scars. Because you will undoubtedly have some, so you need an answer for it. This is one test you cannot skip.

We also need a theology of scars because every society, every people group, and every religion has one. Even continents have different theologies of pain. Americans think about pain drastically differently than East Africans or those in the Middle East.

So if every kingdom has an answer, what is ours? What is the Kingdom of Jesus' answer?

The theme of pain and suffering in the Bible is not some random topic mentioned a few times, no, it is a major theme of the biblical narrative and of the life of a Christian. When we look at suffering, biblically, we see that suffering itself is used 167 times in the Old Testament and dozens of times in the New Testament.

The words suffer, endure, hardship, and affliction are seen throughout the entirety of the Scriptures. The word "suffering" in the Hebrew and the Greek has the idea to take upon one's self a crisis, to endure sorrow, reproach, pain (both emotionally and physically), to be afflicted or pressed, or to suffer under the hand of another; to be the recipient of the blows of faith, to suffer misfortune, the idea of multiplicity of experiences which can overtake a man; to experience something which comes from without, something encounters us and comes upon us without our request or without warning. The Latin word for suffering comes from two words which mean to under-go. It means to yield to, and endure the pain that one is under.

The Bible clearly shows us that we can suffer for Christ or with Christ, to suffer punishment, to be evilly treated, to suffer adversity, to suffer wrongfully, to suffer hardship, trouble, loss, persecution, to receive an impression or be marked by suffering.

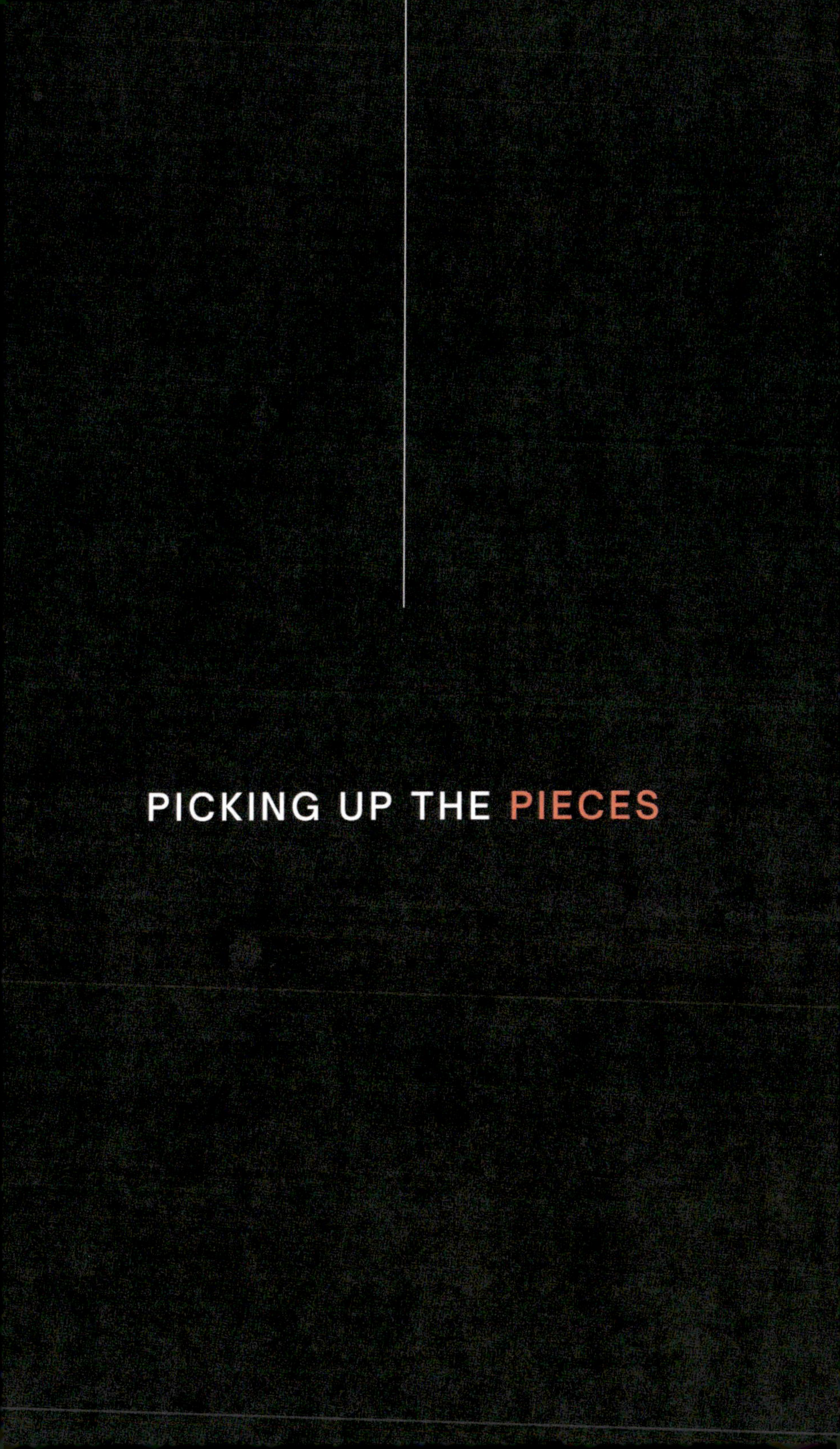
PICKING UP THE PIECES

Am I the only one with a heart that hurts? Am I the only one who has experienced unfair and unjust pain over the last couple years? I don't think so. No, I know so. Maybe you are holding this book in your hand with tears streaming down your face because while you have been reading, all you have been thinking is "me too." I hope as you are reading these words, it's giving you the power to name something, to name your pain. I also hope these words are giving you comfort knowing you aren't alone.

This book is dedicated to my dad. 10 years ago my dad was diagnosed with cancer in both sides of his hip. While he was battling cancer and doing all of his chemotherapy, 300 hours of it to be exact, he had one doctor that he really liked. At the end of all his treatments, and they declared him cancer free, he had one final meeting with his doctor. As they talked through the last 12 months of appointments, chemo, tests, etc., they also talked about the future. What would it look like, and what does this mean moving forward? In the conversation my dad had just found out the damage the chemo had done to his body, specifically his hip, and that he would be in pain for the rest of his life. He would have trouble moving, forever. Talk about devastation. You beat cancer, you finally finish all the chemo and radiation, and then are told you will have very little mobility the rest of your life. My dad asked her one simple question, " What do you expect me to do now?" And her response back was kind, but quick. "Pick up the pieces you have left, and build the best life you possibly can."

I want to prophetically borrow that doctor's words and write them on your heart. If you are holding this book in your hand, and you are either in a season of unbelievable pain, or possibly did a few years ago and the shrapnel is still very present, and you have the same question as my dad, I want to say the same words to you: pick up the pieces.

Pick up the remaining pieces, and build the best life you possibly can.

You could be holding the pieces of your life right now and it looks shattered and unredeemable. But it is. It is redeemable. It is a life worth living. Some of those pieces you lost are not coming back, I know, but there is something beautiful God is trying to do in the midst of it. If you will let Him.

As we prepare to get deeper into this book, I want to forewarn all those who continue on this journey. The next pages you will read, it is going to be about Jesus and the biblical view of pain and suffering.

Maybe you are not a spiritual or religious person at all and your friend gave you this book knowing it might help your current season. Maybe you were scrolling on your kindle and the title was interesting to you. Or maybe you are a follower of Jesus, currently mad at God for the injustice and pain you are seeing and experiencing. Welcome to this journey.

Why Jesus and the Bible? Because it's the greatest, I believe, answer to the pain in the world and the pain in your heart. Not secularism, not New Age spirituality, not self-help seminars, and for sure not getting more control in your life. The person of Jesus and the biblical narrative is the greatest answer we possess on the earth.

The brilliant CS Lewis says "*Christianity, if false, is of no importance. If true, of infinite importance. The only thing it cannot be is moderately important.*"

He goes on to say *"If there is no such thing as water, then why are we all thirsty. If nothing in this world satisfies us, it shows that we are made for another."*

If you are reading this book and you are not a follower of Jesus, I invite you to consider Him. If
you are one, Jesus is inviting you into deeper intimacy with Him.

Let us go on a journey together, whether a skeptic or a disciple. Give me a chance to show you a theology of scars. Let's talk about what to do with a bleeding heart. How to walk again after the rug of life has been yanked out from under you. And most importantly, to consider what Jesus of Nazareth tells us to do with all the pain, loss, and anger life has dealt.

PART ONE

a theology of *scars*

WHERE ARE YOU?

There is much debate out there about what book of the Bible is the most important to read. In my view, hands down, it's Genesis.. It's my favorite book in the Bible and in my opinion the most important to know. If you don't have a firm grasp on the book of Genesis, then the rest of the Bible is going to be a bit blurry. Why Genesis? Because if you don't know how we got here, why we are here, or how things went wrong, then understanding the rest of the story is going to be difficult or misinterpreted.

The first three chapters of the Bible are some of the most important chapters in the all 66 books. They are the stories of creation, the character of Yahweh, the first humans: Adam and Eve, the devil's agenda, and how this all went horribly wrong.

I want to springboard our discussion off these verses below. I realize there's several of them, but stay with me and read them carefully.

"Now the serpent was more crafty than any of the wild animals the Lord God had made. He said to the woman, "Did God really say, 'You must not eat from any tree in the garden'?" 2 The woman said to the serpent, "We may eat fruit from the trees in the garden, 3 but God did say, 'You must not eat fruit from the tree that is in the middle of the garden, and you must not touch it, or you will die.'" 4 "You will not certainly die," the serpent

*said to the woman. 5 "For God knows that when you eat from it your eyes will be opened, and you will be like God, knowing good and evil." 6 When the woman saw that the fruit of the tree was good for food and pleasing to the eye, and also desirable for gaining wisdom, she took some and ate it. She also gave some to her husband, who was with her, and he ate it. 7 Then the eyes of both of them were opened, and they realized they were naked; so they sewed fig leaves together and made coverings for themselves. 8 Then the man and his wife heard the sound of the Lord God as he was walking in the garden in the cool of the day, and they hid from the Lord God among the trees of the garden. 9 But the Lord God called to the man, "Where are you?" 10 He answered, "I heard you in the garden, and I was afraid because I was naked; so I hid" (**Gen 3:1-10** NIV).*

I know I know, stay with me. There is A LOT in those few verses, as there is in the whole of the first three chapters. No, we aren't going to tackle the idea of a talking snake, no, we don't have time to scientifically argue the creation of the world, and yes, the judgment of God is hard to process. All those fun topics are for another book and another conversation.

For now I want you to see what happens in a seemingly simple but incredibly profound conversation between God and Adam.

To recap the story so we are all on the same page. God made Adam and Eve and placed them in a garden. By the way—God does not create anything out of boredom or lack, but out of love. Including you. That Garden is called Eden, and in Hebrew that word Eden is "paradise or delight." That's right, God's entire idea and plan for humanity is for us to live with Him in paradise.

In the garden there were animals, trees, mountains, rivers, friendship, sex, glorious work to be done furthering the garden, God himself, and all of this was available to these humans. But there was one thing God said 'no' to. Yes, even in paradise there are boundaries. A place with no boundaries and no restraint is not freedom, it's bondage. God said, "Do not eat of the tree of the knowledge of good and evil."

Of course, like all humans when they are told not to do something, they are drawn to do that very thing. Adam and Eve eat of the tree of the knowledge of good and evil. They disobey God's commands, and they realize they are naked for the first time. So they hid in the trees and dressed themselves with fig leaves. They were the first 'naked and afraid' long before the TV Show ever came out. Side note: Isn't it funny how Adam and Eve worshipped the tree so deeply, that when they disobeyed God's command they dressed themselves in leaves from that tree? Why? Because you will always end up looking like the thing you worship.

They clothe themselves in fig leaves and they hide. And then God shows up walking in the cool of the day and he asks a bizarre question to Adam. “Where are you?” Wait...what? That’s God’s first words after Adam and Eve ruin paradise? A question? And a weird one at that.

Is Adam really good at hide and seek or something? Is God not all-knowing and He actually doesn’t know where they are hiding? Well of course not. Of course God knows where Adam is. God in absolute generosity is giving Adam a chance to confess.

If you are a parent of a young child, you do this too. When you’ve said no to the cookies on the counter but then see your toddler trying to climb on top of said counter to get said cookies, you ask, “What are you doing?” It’s not because you don’t know; you are watching them doing it and you are giving them a chance to change their actions.

God is asking Adam “Where are you?” not because God doesn’t know where Adam is; He is seeing if Adam knows where he is.

I believe God is asking many of you right now the same question. Where are you? Do you know? Maybe like myself as I was in the middle of that worship service, you actually haven't slowed down enough to think and take inventory of your own soul to know where you are, who you are, or what is going on in your heart.

St Augustine of Hippo in the 4th century famously said in his writings Confessions, "*How can you draw close to God when you are far from your own self? Grant me, Oh Lord, that I may know thyself so that I might know you greater.*"

How's your heart? Right now.

Anxious.

Worried.

Angry.

Distant.

Sad.

Up until that night when this all started, I didn't know where I was. I had no idea what was building under the surface. I was really good at compartmentalization, and any area of my life I didn't feel like addressing, I was able to put aside and keep focusing on the other good areas.

I don't know if you know this, I know this is very revelatory, but ignoring things doesn't make them go away. Yes I know, profound.

What happened that night in that worship service, I was able to finally identify the state of my heart. To finally identify where I was, and this willingness to yield to the Holy Spirit changed everything.

The state of the human heart is a core theme in the Bible and a major concern to God. To the ancient mind, the heart is not the thing beating in your chest. It is the seat of your very being. It's who you are. Your soul, heart and mind, are essentially all the same thing to the early Hebrew minds. It's your inner world, your very being. Your heart was not the life source, but the source of life. How you think, how you feel, why you do certain things: it's your heart. And it matters greatly to God.

So much so, that if you do the right action but with the wrong heart, God doesn't want it. Seriously, think about that. God doesn't want your deeds if your heart isn't it. God is not just a lip reader, more than that, he is a heart reader.

The state of your heart is not a side issue in scripture, it is a massive core motif.

Weirdly enough in the Hebrew language, the word for soul, “neseph” means both soul and throat. How is that possible? I know it’s really weird, because that doesn’t make sense in the English language. How could that word mean those two things, they have nothing in common. Well, the Hebrew language is very different from the English language.

The Hebrew language made them the same word because they have the same function. What goes in and out of your throat, like water and food, is a matter of life and death. Same with your soul, what goes in and out of it is a matter of life and death. It is your Neseph. For example if you allow unhealthy food to pass through your throat into your body, it is going to affect your physical health. Same with your soul, if you allow unhealthy relationships, mindsets, or behaviors to pass through your soul into your life, it will affect your spiritual body.

This is why life itself can be flourishing all around you in every category, but if your heart and soul are not well, it makes everything else suffer. Maybe in times past you have looked at your life and you are just crushing it financially, yet you are sad and depressed and not doing well. And you don’t understand why, because you finally got the stuff you have been grinding for, yet it didn't fix the hole you feel inside your heart.

That's because the most important thing about you is the health of your soul, not the health of your 401k.

As Jesus famously said in Mark 8:36, *"what profits a man to gain the whole world, but lose his soul"*

Notice when you ask someone, especially someone in the western part of the world, how you are doing, they answer with life details. Work, kids, marriage, travel, investments, relationships, etc. Why? Because most westerners think of the 'you' in the sentence 'how are *you* doing,' is your life. Not you, your heart and soul.

So many times we don't even know how to answer the question about our inner world, so we can only answer it about our outward world. So this question of where are you, is of the utmost importance.

When I asked the question "where are you?" I'm not talking about where are you in life, where are you in your career, I am asking do you know where *you* are, where is your soul. How is your soul?

Is it crushed, is it weary, is it broken?

If your heart hurts I got good news for you. *Ps 34:18 promises that "God is close to the broken hearted."*

By the way, it's okay to be reading this and your life is amazing and more than you could ever ask for. No pain or loss currently working itself through your world. Just put this little book in your back pocket when life comes knocking. I encourage you to use this as a guide to help you be there for those around you who are in deep pain.

If you read the rest of that Genesis story in Chapter 3, you will see how good this God is. When Adam and Eve admit they are naked, God kills an animal and makes clothing and covers them. God's heart is to always cover. Protect. Love. But God can't cover what you refuse to confess. You must admit where you are and what you are.

I have been in full time ministry, working for a local church, for the last 15 years of my life. I don't even know how many pastoral conversations I have had. Hundreds and hundreds. I can't tell you how many times this phrase has been said to me "I don't know how I got here." That phrase is usually coming from someone who just shipwrecked their life or made a decision they greatly regret. And they are waking up one day and realizing they have been drifting unknowingly for months and months, sometimes years.

You know what's interesting, out of all of those conversations I have never met with someone and they accidentally drifted into a good marriage. Accidentally drifted into their dream life. Accidentally drifted into deep meaningful relationships. No, that doesn't happen, life doesn't work that way. You always drift away from where you want to be. You go on autopilot, you don't take the time to sit and ask yourself; where am I, and what is the state of my soul and my life.

In this garden called life, where are you right now, in this moment?

The great AW Tozer says in The Pursuit of God, *"The unattended garden will soon be overrun with weeds; the heart that fails to cultivate truth and root out error will shortly be a theological wilderness."*

This might be a good moment in our journey to put the book down for a few minutes. Take a deep breath and find out. We serve a Father in heaven that searches for his children when they are hiding.

If you don't know where you are and you are currently so out of touch on what is truly going on with you. Pray this psalm:

Psalm 139:23-24

"Search me, O God, and know my heart; test me and know my anxious thoughts. Point out anything in me that offends you, and lead me along the path of everlasting life"

David literally asks God to show him, himself. Point out anything within me I am not aware of. Sometimes we need help from God to see ourselves truly.

When you begin to ask these deep questions you can sorta feel like you're dealing with a Pandora's box. You have no idea what is going to come out and when. You begin to deep dive into your soul, relive old trauma and pain, slow down enough to recognize your unhappiness. It can be a lot to say the least. It can be very overwhelming. But it is absolutely worth it. It's like the chiropractor, it hurts so good, not in the moment, but the next few days the benefits are there.

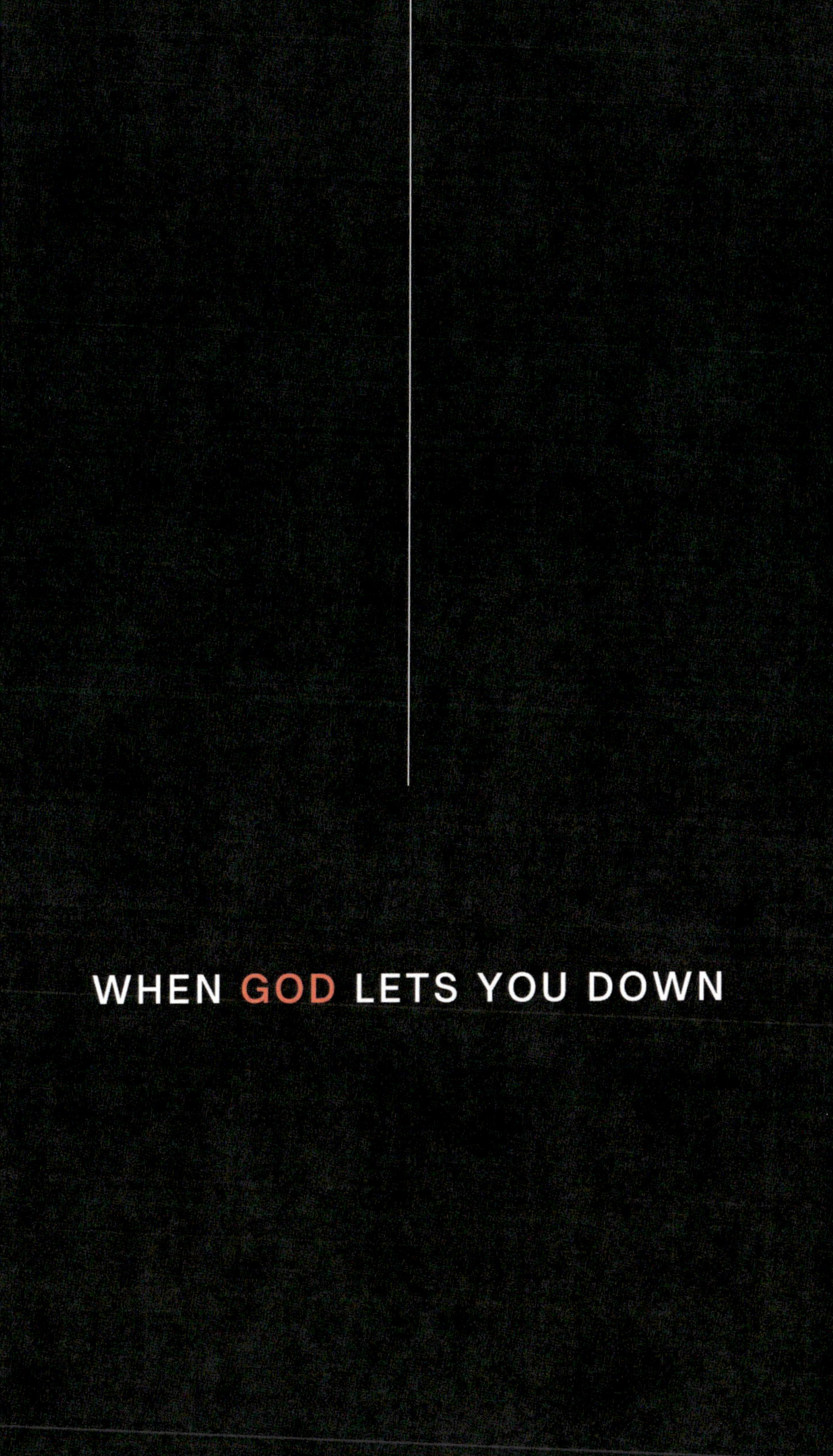
WHEN GOD LETS YOU DOWN

WHERE WAS GOD

This world is a veil of tears and all our technological genius has not been able to dry our tears. It's full of tragedy, suffering, and surprises, that lead people to respond very differently one to another. Some get bitter, some withdraw, others break down mentally, emotionally, or physically. Suffering is a subject we cannot ignore, especially theologically. It raises so many questions in the human heart.

Why is there suffering in the world? Will God do anything about these people who are suffering? What about the doctrine of faith and healing and miracles?

How do we reconcile the Scriptures on God answering prayer and then people dying after

we pray for them, with no evidence of healing?

Even as a pastor, I was struggling. Yes, I was preaching every Sunday, I was leading the staff to the best of my ability, but I was hurting, deeply. I was leading with a broken heart. During that season of excruciating pain that I described earlier, God and I really had words.

Where are you?

Why aren't you stepping in?

I had absolute faith for that healing, why didn't you do it?

How can this much evil be present in the life of a believer?

I was quoting God's words back to him, scripture after scripture.

Yet the pain remained.

These sentiments aren't new of course. It's the age-old reason why people aren't religious.

"I wont believe in a God that lets evil persist in the world"

For most people who are atheist, agnostic, or those who want nothing to do with God or church, that statement is the threshing floor. That statement is the barrier. People cannot get past the injustice, evil, sexual abuse, murder, racism, hurricanes, and cancer in the world while a "loving God" stands by and watches. Why didn't God do anything? Why didn't he step in and stop it? Where was God?

One day I saw this bumper sticker on a car in downtown Portland:

"God is all powerful. God is good. There is evil in the world. Pick two."

That bumper sticker is it. That sentence right there is the heart beat of so many. They do not understand how Christian's can believe these two truths simultaneously: God is good and God is all powerful. How can that sentence be true?

If we are to belong to God and we serve God, we must understand who the God of the Bible is. Knowing and trusting the nature of God is essential if we are to suffer with a Godly attitude and receive maximum benefit from the school of suffering. We need to understand both the essential attributes and the moral attributes.

God is just and God is right. The word "just" has the idea of one who proportions exactly right, one who observes divine laws without breaking those laws: one who is such as he "ought to be at all times" and in every situation, meaning he is upright; one who is faultless, always fair; one who renders to each his due, passing just judgment on all.

He makes things right with equity, He is equitable in His distribution of justice. He is called the Just Judge, He is impartial. He judges with integrity and virtue and He exists with this integrity to give His judgment to every living creature. God can never give to someone something that is unjust. God is always just, God is always right, and God is always fair.

Those sentences are incredibly hard to believe. I believe them in my head, but my heart has a hard time with those words.

Author Chuck Swindoll says in Insights for Living, *"God's mysteries, especially suffering, defy human explanation because they go beyond human intellect and wisdom. We lack eternal perspective. We cannot grasp God's plan. But we can say with Job, 'Though I am without answers, yet I will believe in Him".*

You and I have an interesting relationship with pain don't we. Because there are different levels of it and different reasons for it. The way I see it, and I could be wrong, but I think there are three different relationships we have with pain.

1 CHOSEN PAIN

Think about it, people will pay for pain. I have a lot of tattoos, and tattoos are painful. I have paid a good amount of money for someone to hurt me. People will pay for a painful back surgery, go through incredibly painful physical therapy, but know it will be beneficial in the long term. People put themselves through excruciating workouts that hurt and wear out their bodies, but they see the benefit. People put themselves through excruciating workouts, but know there is a reward on the other side. People choose to end relationships, though it's painful, they initiate the difficulty by ending the relationship.

We can handle chosen pain.

2 DESERVED PAIN

Though we didn't want it, didn't choose it, we are subconsciously okay when pain enters our life if we think we deserve it. "Well, I brought it upon myself, it's my fault" we tell ourselves and others. We have a weird acceptance level of horrible pain if we think we deserve it, because well, who else could we blame? There is no one else to point the finger at, so I guess I will just suck it up and be okay with it. We then say things like, "I deserved this, but I am going to learn from it, I won't let this happen again." Chosen pain and deserved pain have one thing in common: we tend to believe there is a purpose for it.

We can handle deserved pain.

3 UNJUST PAIN

This. This we cannot handle. This pain is the 6-month old dying of SIDS, the hurricanes that kill thousands of people, people dying of hunger around the world, and the list could go on and on. We can intellectually process chosen pain and deserved pain, but we cannot with unjust pain. It's unfair. Our soul groans with a sense that the world should not be like this. This is not right. This is where we draw the line on the idea of God's goodness and power.

Have you noticed we tend to not ask the question "Where was God" with the first 2 categories. It's only unjust pain to which we begin asking this question. Where does that come from? Where does the idea of justice and injustice come from?

If there is no God, if the universe was an accident of atoms and cells running into each other, where do humans get the idea of right and wrong, justice and injustice?

The idea of justice is baked into the human DNA, even from infancy. Have you been at a park lately overrun with toddlers? It's like *Lord of the Flies* out there. Who gets the slide, who gets the swing, who gets the monkey bars, and what happens when a 3-year old thinks it's her turn and a 4-year old cuts them in line?

"IT'S MY TURN. THAT'S UNFAIR" the toddler yells. Wait...fair? How does a child already have a sense of fair and unfair. How does a toddler already know, when something unjust happens, a sense rises out of their soul "this is not how the world is supposed to be."

Where does that come from? God. That comes from your creator. Because you were made in the image of God, who is a God of justice, it's in you to want the same. This is why we can't comprehend unjust pain. I believe death is so hard for humans to swallow for one simple reason: we weren't meant to.

In the Genesis story we were made to live in the garden with God forever. We could have eaten from the tree of life and lived with God in paradise forever. But sin ruined that, and now we can taste death. I believe the reason why humans have such a hard time with injustice is because we were never made to taste it. It's a meal we don't have a palate for.

However, and here is the key, when pain finds its purpose, even unjust pain,It changes everything.

The world renowned author and survivor of the holocaust, Viktor Frankl, said, *"Everything can be taken from a man, but one thing. The last of human freedoms: to choose one's attitude in any given set of circumstances, to choose one's own way."*

In some ways suffering ceases to be suffering at the moment it finds a meaning. Life is never made unbearable by circumstances, but only by lack of meaning and purpose. People have the means to live, but no meaning to live for. The lack of purpose adds another level of weight upon the weight that suffering has already brought. When life seems unfair, pain is continuing to pile up and when it seems like it is for no reason, it becomes unbearable. If you could find the purpose within the moment, it will give you the strength to put one more foot in front of the other. To fight for one more day. But in order for us to find purpose in it, we need a better theology

A BETTER THEOLOGY

Christendom is a kinda confusing world. There are so many different denominations and sectors of Christianity. Lutheran, Presbyterian, Catholic, Charismatic, eastern orthodoxy, Baptist, to name just a few. I was raised in the more evangelical and charismatic movements in the church world. I know only a little bit about all those other movements and spheres, but I think I am on safe grounds to make this statement: Christians, no matter their denominations or sector, have not done the best job answering and handling pain and suffering in the church. Pain and suffering can get very nuanced when God's name and God's will are involved.

I was 26 when my dad got diagnosed with cancer, we just had our first son, I believe Cruz was 6months old. My boss at the church and my dads best friend had just died of ALS a few months before my dad got sick.

My head was spinning. I didn't know who to talk to, how to process it, or really what to do. During that season the amount of relational and spiritual "advice" I was giving was overwhelming. What to do when my dad dies, how to talk to God in thankfulness for the honor of suffering for him, how to lead my home through crisis, how to pastor well, etc etc.

After about 3 months of the overwhelming data I was given and post cards in the mail, all I remember thinking, even at 26, was: we need a better answer to people's pain. Is this really how we respond to crises and disasters?

We must get a better theology around suffering. I didn't know what the answer was, but I knew what I was experiencing wasn't it. Perhaps you're familiar with some of the theology out there:

If you would have prayed more, God would have showed up.

If you just had more faith they would have been healed

Don't confess that over your body, confess you are healed

Well if they die at least they are in a better place

Ever heard those sentences? Ever been told those things in a church hallway by a well meaning elder?

I have. Many times.

I remember when my dad was going through his chemo treatments, a well meaning elder wanted to talk to me in the hallway. He pulled me aside and asked me to stop saying my dad had cancer, and start declaring he is healed. “But he does have cancer” I said back, kinda confused. They retorted back, “Only because you keep saying that, don’t confess that! start saying he is healed!” I just stared and smiled and thought to myself....this isn’t helpful.

Unfortunately for too long have Christians have given shallow answers to deep questions. Quick off-the-cuff statements instead of long, deep, difficult, conversations.

It’s not because they are evil people, it’s not because they don’t mean well or even because they don’t love God.

It’s because, for many of us, we were given a poor theology of scars. As Christians, many of us just don’t know what to do with pain through the lenses of a loving God.

One of the worst theologies floating around in the world of doctrine is that all pain is the result of sin. You hear it in people’s tone, you sense it in their questions. When it is announced that someone is going through something horrific, people subtly wonder or even ask “so.... what did they do? I wonder what God is dealing with them about”

That doctrine falls apart quickly because if you believe that, Jesus must have sinned a lot. Reading the life of

Jesus should shatter that notion. Reading the life of The Apostle Paul should shake you to your core.

Why?

Because their lives show that you can be in the middle of the perfect will of God, and be in pain. Maybe the very reason you are in pain is because you actually said yes to God, not no to God.
If scars from suffering are so wrong, so sinful, then why did Jesus keep his?

Think about it. Jesus' body was absolutely destroyed during his crucifixion. Some scholars say his body was so abused you couldn't tell him from a human or an animal. Some historians say because of the lashing his back endured, most likely his organs were exposed.

Think about those scars.

And yet when Jesus resurrects from the dead, he is now in his heavenly perfected body, and he tells Thomas to touch his scars. Wait....what? Wouldn't you think that in our new heavenly perfected body we would be made whole and perfect, no scars no blemishes. Not Jesus. He kept his scars.

Yes heaven is a place where there is no suffering, no tears, but that doesn't mean it's a place with no scars. Oh yes, there will be scars.

You see, we need to stop running from the conversation of pain and suffering. We need to embrace it. Because it's such a massive part of the human experience. It's what makes us who we are. There are some aspects of your character only valleys can make, not the mountain tops. I would venture to say that some of your heroes, the thing you love about them, pain created it.

In his book, "Don't Waste Your Sorrows" Dr. Bilhymer states, *"Because tribulation is necessary for the decentralization of self and the development of deep dimensions of agape love, this love can only be developed in the school of suffering. The greatest saints are the greatest sufferers."*

CS Lewis writes in *The Problem with Pain—"I suggest to you that it is because God loves us that he gives us the gift of suffering. Pain is God's megaphone to a deaf world. You see, we are blocks of stone out of which the Sculptor carves the forms of men. The blows of his chisel, which hurt so much, are what makes us perfect"*

Could those statements be true? Yes I believe so. Because no one leaves a season of suffering the same. You will change. You just get to choose how.

Have you ever heard the old adage from Charles Spurgeon *"the same sun that melts the snow is the same sun that hardens the mud"*

I submit, the same pain that melts some people hardens others. Pain is not neutral, it will change you. But in what way? You have met these people. Life made them mean and harsh, cold and distant, and others it made them thankful, soft and kind, generous and merciful.

What does heat do? It either refines or it melts. I pray that the heat from the pain in your life refines you, it molds you, it reshapes you. Into a person pure as gold.

Knock knock. Jesus is waiting at your door again. Waiting to be let in, to walk with you through your pain and suffering.

The late Tim Keller said in a sermon – *"God wants to walk with you through your pain. Not sit with you, that leads to depression. Not run with you, that leads to lack of growth. But walk with you through it"*

You must understand that for followers of Jesus prayer is not where we go to escape reality. It's where we go to face it. We must not treat prayer as some alter-reality that we run to, to hide from the world and act like everything is perfect. Sometimes prayer is the place Christians go to lie to themselves, not face themselves.

Prayer should be the place we go to talk to God, in total honesty, and face life. Face the pain.

I personally don't understand how the Church at large got so lost in her answer to pain and suffering. To ignore this theme is to ignore much of the Bible. If you spend any length of time reading the scriptures, it is filled with people experiencing injustice. I mean for most Christians the psalms are their favorite verses and prayers, and yet 1/3 of the psalms are prayers of lament.

Pain is not a random detail in a few verses in obscure books, it is a massive motif in the narrative of the Bible cover to cover.

We must find a better way forward.

BLINDING PAIN

When my sister Bethany passed away, for a month or so afterward I was in an emotional wilderness. I didn't know how I felt, what I was feeling or not feeling, every day was a different emotion. Without going into unnecessary details, simply put, I had a very unique relationship with Bethany.

My parents were told they would never have kids and that life-dream wasn't in the cards for them. They continued trying in faith for 12 years, to no avail. After 12 years they decided to adopt a girl from Guatemala, my oldest sister Nicole. A few years later, they adopted another girl from Oregon, my other older sister Bethany. Four years after that, they miraculously got pregnant with me, and then five years after that, again miraculously pregnancy with my little sister Jessica. So I am the only boy, and in the middle of two adopted siblings and one younger biological one.

Bethany was incredibly intelligent, and went to college for an English major while getting straight As and earning the Dean's List. She was very witty with a high vocabulary, so while she was ripping you to shreds, you were laughing, not knowing she was telling you how unintelligent you were. She liked quirky shows like Beavis and Butt-head and King of the Hill, you know the good ol 90s wholesome TV shows pastor kids would watch while their parents were at elder meetings. I have a lot of funny memories of us teaming up to do things we should not be doing. But, unfortunately those memories aren't the majority of my memories.

A good portion of my childhood memories with Bethany are vivid days and moments of her struggling with being adopted. She could not wrap her mind around someone 'not wanting her' and giving her up for adoption. I remember her frequently packing her bags to run away from home to find her biological mom and to look for her "real family." Throughout middle school and high school she would try and find her biological mother, look her up in the yellow pages (remember those) and online adoption sites, yet she never could find her. So though she lived in a loving home with two parents and three siblings, it wasn't filling the hole she felt in her heart.

This hole in her heart would begin to cause deep deep damage, physically and emotionally. She got into some unhealthy relationships and friend groups which led to drugs and alcohol, checking in and out of rehabs for the next 15 years of her life. After being an addict for almost 10 years of her life, she finally got sober and started turning her life around.

She started coming to our church that we just launched, and she was there every Sunday night. My oldest son,

Cruz, would go to my parents' house with her and build these 2,000 piece lego sets for hours and hours.

But then Covid hit, and the lock down affected her deeply: she sank into a deep depression and did not leave her room. She started drinking again heavily, and she ended up drinking herself to death in her apartment.

When we went to clean out her apartment, we found a suitcase full of notes and letters she would write to herself. Many of the letters spoke about that ever present hole in her heart about not having a "real family"

Why do I say all of this? She possessed what she was searching for, she had a family, she had parents, she had siblings. Bethany spent a good portion of her life looking for something she already had.

Pain can blind you. It can distort your vision. There is some pain that is so deep and so crushing, it blinds you to the reality sitting in front of you.

Saint Oscar Romero said, "There are many things that can only be seen through eyes that have cried."

Pain will inevitably change your vision. You just get to choose how. Will it blind your vision or enhance your vision?

Of course—there are many people reading this that can identify times in your life when this has happened: when one thing in your life absolutely distorted your perspective of the rest of your life. Bethany experienced something that another man in the Bible experienced, in his moment of pain. This man is called John the Baptist, this man is Jesus' cousin.

If you have ever read the Bible, toward the middle-right are these four books that we call the Gospels. Matthew, Mark, Luke and John. It's the four books we have about the life of Jesus, from birth to ascension back to heaven. Sometimes I think modern Christians only read the stories we like, ones we can understand or the ones we agree with. Therefore we end up with "my Jesus" theology. We say things like "well my Jesus would never do that. My Jesus would never have those types of rules". By doing this we end up with a pseudo version of ourselves that we feel comfortable following and we call that ideal Jesus.

There are some parables Jesus teaches that are unbelievably difficult to process. Jesus is not always the soft and kind rabbi, sometimes he says some absurd things that we must wrestle with. Furthermore there are a few stories in there that are really hard to reconcile, even with his best friends. This is one of those stories, it does not go how we think it should go.

Matthew 11:1-15 *"After Jesus had finished instructing his twelve disciples, he went on from there to teach and preach in the towns of Galilee.* ***2*** *When John, who was in prison, heard about the deeds of the Messiah, he sent his disciples* ***3*** *to ask him, "Are you the one who is to come, or should we expect someone else?"****4*** *Jesus replied, "Go back and report to John what you hear and see:* ***5*** *The blind receive sight, the lame walk, those who have leprosy are cleansed, the deaf hear, the dead are raised, and the good news is proclaimed to the poor.* ***6*** *Blessed is anyone who does not stumble on account of me."* ***7*** *As John's disciples were leaving, Jesus began to speak to the crowd about John: "What did you go out into the wilderness to see? A reed swayed by the wind?* ***8*** *If not, what did you go out to see? A man dressed in fine clothes? No, those who wear fine clothes are in kings' palaces.* ***9*** *Then what did you go out to see? A prophet? Yes, I tell you, and more than a prophet.* ***10*** *This is the one about whom it is written:*

> *"'I will send my messenger ahead of you,*
> *who will prepare your way before you.'*

11 *Truly I tell you, among those born of women there has not risen anyone greater than John the Baptist; yet whoever is least in the kingdom of heaven is greater than he.* ***12*** *From the days of John the Baptist until now, the kingdom of heaven has been subjected to violence,* *and violent people have been raiding it.* ***13*** *For all the Prophets and the Law prophesied until John.* ***14*** *And if you are willing to accept it, he is the Elijah who was to come.* ***15*** *Whoever has ears, let them hear"*

....What just happened. That can't be the loving Jesus I know. Why didn't Jesus go rescue him? John the Baptist surely didn't mean that? The man who has been preaching and teaching, baptizing people in the name of God, is now asking is Jesus the one? Is now questioning his faith in Jesus?

Let's unpack this together.

Jesus has come fully into his ministry, he is preaching and teaching, healing people, and shaking the Roman Empire to its core. Some people like Jesus but most do not.

John the Baptist is Jesus' cousin, and one of the major characters in the New Testament during the life of Jesus. He preached about the gospel of the Kingdom and he was the guy who proclaimed that the messiah of the world was coming. Long story short this gets John the Baptist thrown into prison to be beheaded. He is sitting in a Roman prison waiting to be executed.

He gathers some of his friends and essentially asks them for a final favor. Can you go find Jesus for me and ask him a question. His friends are nodding, but what comes next they were not expecting. John the baptist goes on to say "Ask him if he is the one I have been waiting for or is there another". I don't think I can fully describe to you the magnitude and the weight of that question, and the underlying unrest it must have brought to the hearers.

When you read the history of John the baptist, his miraculous birth, his calling in this life, trained by his mom and dad who were righteous people, after 30 years of 'making the way' for the son of God. For 30 years he had been preaching about a man that is coming to reconcile the world, and now he is second guessing this very man?

This moment is deeply profound.

Jesus gets the message from John's friends and he says back, "*Go back and report to John what you hear and see: The blind receive sight, the lame walk, those who have leprosy are cleansed, the deaf hear, the dead are raised, and the good news is proclaimed to the poor. Blessed is anyone who does not stumble on account of me.*"

AKA Jesus is saying, John I'm not coming to get you, but don't worry the gospel is being preached, the lame walk, the deaf hear. John, I am who you were waiting for and I'm not coming to rescue you.

How has John gone from preaching boldly about the name of Jesus to now questioning everything...What happened?

Pain and Suffering happened. That's what happened.

His pain was blinding. His vision of Jesus and his Kingdom was distorted.

He is sitting in prison waiting to be beheaded for this Jesus. And he is thinking "was it worth it? Is he the one?" Could you imagine John sitting in prison about to die just waiting for a good response from Jesus, and it doesn't come.

How many times in your life have you felt like John the Baptist? "For real Jesus. You aren't going to come save me? After all I have done for you, you aren't going to rescue me from this prison?"

It's so hard to trust in Jesus when he doesn't do it the way you thought he would. Do you see Jesus' response? It's absolutely mind blowing. He essentially says, John don't worry! I am who you think I am, I am healing the blind and healing the deaf, the gospel is being preached! And you are still going to die, but I am still true to my word.

This is hard to wrestle with.

By the way—This is the goal of the enemy of your soul, Satan, to take pain and suffering and use it to make you question who God is.

How many people do you know that have walked away because of suffering? People who walked away from their church community, their faith, and ultimately God himself. It's the family members, co-workers, best friends from college that grew up in church, who experienced great pain and deconstructed their beliefs and walked away.

Probably a good amount.

The craziest part of the entire story, at least to me, is this next part. Use your imagination to envision this scene.

Jesus is in the middle of a sermon. John's friends come and interrupt him. And they say hey, your cousin is in prison and he is going to die soon. He just wants to know before he dies if you are the one he has been waiting for, if you are worth it for him to die for.

You would think Jesus' response would be an outrage... WHAT! HE IS SECOND GUESSING ME!? AFTER ALL THOSE SERMONS AND BAPTISMS HE HAS PERFORMED!

No, Jesus isn't like that.

Jesus doesn't act like us. He doesn't disown John, he doesn't cancel him and call him a sell out. He talks to the crowd about how amazing John is and how he is one of the greatest men to walk the face of the earth.

This is the Jesus you serve. This is the heart of God. When you doubt him, he doesn't doubt you. When you second guess him, he doubles down on his love for you.

If your current response to Jesus is "I will only obey you when it makes sense to me and I understand it", that is not obedience that is agreement. It takes obedience to follow Jesus when you don't really want to and you don't understand.

Does your faith hinge on your understanding and agreeing? Are you able to follow even when you kind of doubt and have questions, because doubt is a part of human nature and also a part of the Christian journey.

Jesus is not scared of your doubt. He is not scared of your deep deep emotions about your pain and suffering. He's not even mad when you question Jesus and his absence.

If you are sitting in a prison cell of pain right now, and your heart hurts and your soul feels like it's bleeding out…or maybe you identify and feel just like John the Baptist, asking where Jesus is, are you going to be rescued from this prison, does Jesus even care… I invite you to hear the words of Jesus' friends: He is faithful to his word. He is who you think he is. He is worth it, even when it doesn't happen how you thought.

What has been your theology of scars? Your theology of pain?

You deserve it because of your sin.
God is distant, unloving, and not good.
Life is unfair and karma sucks.
God is really loving but He is not in control.
This is all for God's glory so smile and be thankful.

Any of those sound familiar?

Right now might be a really good moment for you to sit and ponder how you even got your mindset around pain, who gave it to you and if it is working. If you are a

Jesus follower, a more important question is, did Jesus give me this mindset or did someone else?

If following Jesus was an automatic pass on a life of pain and suffering, everyone would be a Christian by now. If claiming the name of Jesus meant life couldn't touch you and now you will experience bliss on earth, we would lose our witness to a hurting world.

In Paul's letter to the believers in Thesselonica, he writes to them about suffering because their loved ones were being martyred for claiming Jesus and they were grieving.

1 Thess 4:13 says, *"we don't grieve like those with no hope."*

Notice what he doesn't say. He doesn't say "Hey Christian, don't grieve! Smile! It's going to be okay"

No. That's not what he says. He says yes we grieve, we just don't grieve like the world grieves. As Christians, we deeply grieve, but we grieve with hope. You are allowed to grieve while simultaneously holding onto hope.

But how? How do you fight to hold that tension?

You wrestle with God about it.

WRESTLING WITH GOD

Names in the bible are very different than they are in the 21st century. Not just the wild names themselves in the Bible like Melchizedek, Ishbi-benob and Nimrod, and yes those are real biblical names, but the meaning and importance of a name. We pick names from popular websites, athletes, and favorite cities in Europe, but that is not the case in 1st century eastern lands.

In the 1st century when you named a child, it was incredibly significant and very prophetic. You typically didn't name a child until they came out of the womb. You would name them based off 3 things:

1. What they looked like. For instance, Esau in the Old Testament name literally means red and hairy, so apparently he came out of the womb very hairy. And that's it, here's your name.
2. How birthing went. For instance in the Old Testament Jabez name means painful birth and full of sorrow. Well I guess that is pretty straight forward, his mother was in so much pain and sorrow after the birth, she named it painful.
3. An insight into their future. If the mother or father was given a dream or vision of what their son would be like in their future, they would name them in hopes they would live up to their name. It was a prophetic declaration over them to a future that was hoped for.

Names were not just names on an ID, they were identities. This is why names were changed so many times in the biblical narrative. Saul to Paul, Abram to Abraham, Cephas to Peter. Because when you meet Jesus, your identity is changed, your name is changed.

In the biblical narrative the nation of God is named Israel. Do you know what their name means? In Hebrew, Israel means "those who struggle with God." That's right, our identity is known as a people who wrestle, fight, and struggle with God. And if you know the Old Testament story very well, you are probably nodding your head and thinking of all the stories and fights between Israel and God.

If you read the 39 books of the Old Testament, it is a long dramatic story of Israel and God in a unique relationship. It kind of reads like a love letter between two people in an unhealthy relationship.

Sounds like this: Israel loves God, serves him and is faithful to him. A few chapters later, Israel abandons God for another evil god, disobeys everything God said. God gets mad at Israel for her disobedience. Israel receives the consequences of her disobedience. God gets mad at Israel's hard heart, but when Israel cries out for a second chance, he forgives her and rescues her. Israel loves God again, and we are back to the love story.

This is a cycle that happens over and over and over again. Actually there is an entire book that talks about Israel's unhealthy relationship to God and this cycle that never ends. It's called the book of judges. And it shows how this dysfunctional cycle repeats itself over and over, generation after generation.

This is the cycle in Judges: Rebellion—Ruin—Repentance—Rescue—Rest

This is why Israel is named this name. We are a people who wrestle with God. Who love him, we serve him, we get mad at him, we leave him, we come running back. The cycle continues.

The stories of the Old Testament are stories of Israel and God fighting it out. And maybe God has invited you into this same wrestling match.

Look at this wrestling match between God and Jacob in Genesis.

"That night Jacob got up and took his two wives, his two female servants and his eleven sons and crossed the ford of the Jabbok. ***23*** *After he had sent them across the stream, he sent over all his possessions.* ***24*** *So Jacob was left alone, and a man wrestled with him till daybreak.* ***25*** *When the man saw that he could not overpower him, he touched the socket of Jacob's hip so that*

his hip was wrenched as he wrestled with the man. **26** *Then the man said, "Let me go, for it is daybreak."*

But Jacob replied, "I will not let you go unless you bless me."

27 *The man asked him, "What is your name?"*

"Jacob," he answered.

28 *Then the man said, "Your name will no longer be Jacob, but Israel, because you have struggled with God and with humans and have overcome."*

29 *Jacob said, "Please tell me your name."*

But he replied, "Why do you ask my name?" Then he blessed him there.

30 *So Jacob called the place Peniel, saying, "It is because I saw God face to face, and yet my life was spared."*
31 *The sun rose above him as he passed Peniel, and he was limping because of his hip.* **32** *Therefore to this day the Israelites do not eat the tendon attached to the socket of the hip, because the socket of Jacob's hip was touched near the tendon. (**Gen 32:22-32).***

There is so much here to unpack, (it's one of my favorite chapters in the Bible), we just don't have time to talk about all of it. But there are four noteworthy takeaways I want you to see.

1) Have you ever considered that a form of worship is wrestling? That we actually serve a God who wants to be wrestled, not dismissed or ignored?

When we have deep questions about pain and suffering, difficult theological questions we want to yell at God about, he invites us to wrestle him, not to shut up and sit down. "Because I said so" is not God's parenting style.

That's right. When you are unbelievably mad at God, and question his goodness and his character, God is inviting you into a deeply intimate relationship. Have you ever watched a wrestling match? It is awkwardly intimate as you are in very close quarters with the other person, and it only involves 2 people.

Exactly.

One of the ways you personally grow in intimacy with Jesus, is when you wrestle with him. You struggle over concepts and scripture. His will and your will. His way and your way.

And by the way—who initiates this? God does. God approaches Jacob to fight. Jacob was minding his own business, he was not seeking God out. But God was seeking Him out.
Maybe that spiritual agitation you have been feeling is God inviting you into a deep relationship with him.

2) Do you see when God initiates this wrestling match? When Jacob is alone. All of his cattle, family and possessions are across the river. He is alone. Nothing to distract him. When you read the story God has had plenty of chances to do this in the last several chapters. But God waits. He is patient. God finally has him right where he wants him: alone.

Maybe those moments in your life that you felt a bit isolated and alone, it was God drawing you to himself. It was God trying to draw you away from the busyness of the crowd, so that his voice is the only one you hear.

You see, God doesn't always shout, many times he whispers. You and I both know how close you have to be to someone to hear a whisper. I believe God whispers on purpose, if you want to hear him you have to draw close.

By choosing to draw close you are also automatically withdrawing from other voices. By saying yes to God you are now saying no to others.

Isolation is when you are running from something, solitude is when you are running to someone.
I feel that many of you are being invited into solitude with God. Just you and him.

3) notice what happens to Jacob when he is done wrestling with God. It says the Lord touches his hip socket, and he now has a limp for the rest of his life. What an interesting place for God to choose to touch. Not the shoulder, not the knee, not his hands.

Why the hip? God is not random, he picked that location on purpose. I believe it's because the hip affects every aspect of your life. You can't move, sit, walk, turn, or bend without it affecting your hips.

That's what wrestling with God through pain and suffering does. It changes you. It changes how you walk, it changes relationships, it gives you a new language. Pain, it changes you, forever.
Hellen Keller said, "Character cannot be developed in ease and quiet. Only through experience of trial and suffering can the soul be strengthened, ambition inspired, and success achieved."

When I read the Bible and study the men and women within those pages, I see people who wrestled with God. Over death and sorrow, over injustice, over God's decisions to act or not act. In scripture these people are called mighty in faith, righteous and have trust in God, yet when you read their stories, they had huge grievances with God. But yet, they still follow him.

Is there a way to be a whole-hearted believer and follower of Jesus, experience devastating pain and suffering, be disappointed in God and yet still be faithful?

I submit, yes.

Difficult? Oh, more than you could ever imagine.

Is it worth it? Absolutely.

Needed? More than ever.

4) Lastly, did you notice how long they wrestled? Until daybreak. Until a new day was dawning. They apparently wrestled all night long. I deeply sense that people reading this book have given up. It was too painful, the answer took too long, God felt distant, and you quit. You threw in the white towel in the 4th round.

Come back to the wrestling. Come back to the struggle. Wrestle all night if you have to, wrestle until the sun comes up. Because this is what will happen if you keep wrestling, a new day is coming. The dawn of a new season is upon you, just keep fighting. Wrestle through the night, fight through the darkness, until the sun begins to shine upon your face.

To quote the infamous *The Dark Night* movie: *"The night is darkest just before the dawn. And I promise you, the dawn is coming"*

I am praying for every single person who finds themselves in the middle of the night, I pray as you wrestle, a new day is coming. A new season is coming.

You see, this story in Genesis is not a stand alone story. It is one of many stories about men wrestling with God. Psalms is one of the most loved and most read books in the Bible, for sure one of the most tattooed and most quoted. I believe one of the main reasons Psalms is loved by Christians and non alike, people love the raw honesty, emotions, and the dialogue with God.

When you read the verses in Psalms, written by a small handful of authors, a good portion of them being King David, you are reading deep seated emotions. And by the way, many are emotions of anger and sadness. Did you know the largest category of the psalms are verses about lamenting and weeping, 65 of the 150 to be exact. That's almost half the book of psalms. This is why we love them; we see ourselves in them. We see our pain in them. We feel seen and heard in someone else's words.

Look at just a few of these passages from King David

Psalms 42:1-6

1 *As the deer pants for streams of water, so my soul pants for you, my God.*

2 *My soul thirsts for God, for the living God. When can I go and meet with God?*

3 *My tears have been my food day and night, while people say to me all day long, "Where is your God?"* **4** *These things I remember as I pour out my soul: how I used to go to the house of God under the protection of the Mighty One with shouts of joy and praise among the festive throng.* **5** *Why, my soul, are you downcast? Why so disturbed within me? Put your hope in God, for I will yet praise him, my Savior and my God.* **6** *My soul is downcast within me; therefore I will remember you from the land of the Jordan. The heights of Hermon—from Mount Mizar"*

Psalms 13:1-2

***1** How long, Lord? Will you forget me forever? How long will you hide your face from me? **2** How long must I wrestle with my thoughts and day after day have sorrow in my heart? How long will my enemy triumph over me?"*

Psalms 10:1

***1** Why, Lord, do you stand far off? Why do you hide yourself in times of trouble?*

Any of those emotions sound familiar? How many times have you asked the same questions?

There is only one man in all of the Bible that was given the title "A man after God's own heart" and that is King David. I don't know about you, but when I read the psalms I often think "are you allowed to talk to God like that". When God hears King David talking like this, God is not upset, he is thankful and loving toward this honest heart.

Apparently, not only are we allowed to, we are invited to.

In our current cultural moment as I write these pages in 2025, Christian deconstruction has divided the church. Deconstruction is the movement of people who were raised in the church, and have left orthodoxy, left the church, and have for the most part, stopped following

Jesus. Some are attempting to follow Jesus, claiming they do not need the Bible, church, or other Christians, to be a Christian. They would say things like "all I need is my Jesus and my Jesus would never do _____." So they end up creating their own Jesus, which is a pseudo version of themselves and they make an idol out of their intellectual ideals and just call that, Jesus. Though that Jesus is nowhere to be found in the scriptures.

This is not a book on deconstruction, there are enough out there, so we wont dive any further into it. But one of the very real aspects, I believe, of some deconstructing Christians is leaving Jesus and the church because of pain and suffering. This I do want to address, because it is very real and very understandable.

I'm sure, just about every person reading this has had a friend leave the faith because of a tragedy in their life, and they felt like Jesus let them down and so did the church. Maybe the church swept it under the rug and dismissed them, told them to pray more, and they felt God was silent and distant. So they left the faith, thinking God's promises in the Bible are not true. Or maybe they were told this is happening because of past sins, and this is how God's wrath works. Or possibly a list of many other horrible and unhelpful answers Christian's and pastors alike have offered over the centuries.

I think we have lost many people who walked away from the faith, simply because we had bad theology around pain and suffering. I sadly wonder how many would still be in our fellowships or families if we handled pain in more biblically minded and emotionally healthy ways.

Friends, I deeply submit, we need a new theology of scars. And Jesus is going to show us a better way forward.

This book might not ease your pain. It might not answer all the questions you have. You might not even like my answers, theologically or psychologically to your pain. Or this book might be deeply healing for you and redeem some time and memories. Both responses are okay.

I invite you to come and wrestle. Argue with me over the next few chapters. Fight with God over your past or present pain you cannot comprehend or get past. Fight with your own experiences that you have let frame your entire existence.

Let us live up to our name, oh Israel, and be those who struggle with God while remaining faithful.

PART TWO

a garden called *gethsemane*

EMOTIONAL GETHSEMANE

As we begin to wrestle with this idea of pain and suffering from a biblical perspective, we are going on a deep dive into the life of Jesus.

As I stated earlier, if you want to talk about the greatest way to face pain, look no further than Jesus of Nazareth. While walking in the perfect and sinless will of God, he endured more pain and suffering than any human should endure.

We are going to look at a moment in Jesus life that is very well known, but I believe greatly overlooked. In my opinion it's one of the greatest moments of the life of Jesus that we see in all of the gospels. It is by far the most vulnerable and human we see Jesus on this earth. Let me set the scene for you.

This is the last week of Jesus' life. He just had this special moment with his disciples called the last supper, in the upper room. (You can go read in the book of John chapters 13-16 about this) He is saying good-bye to his best friends. It's his last sermon to them before he is brutally crucified. They are saying they understand, but they really don't. They aren't really tracking with what Jesus is saying about his death, burial and resurrection and what must take place.

Judas has left the 12 to betray Jesus. In a few moments he will sell Jesus for 30 pieces of silver to the Roman Empire to be killed.

While Judas is talking to the Roman Empire, Jesus and his disciples take one last walk. To a garden. The garden of Gethsemane.

"Then Jesus went with them to the olive grove called Gethsemane, and he said, "Sit here while I go over there to pray." ***37*** *He took Peter and Zebedee's two sons, James and John, and he became anguished and distressed.* ***38*** *He told them, "My soul is crushed with grief to the point of death. Stay here and keep watch with me."*

39 *He went on a little farther and bowed with his face to the ground, praying, "My Father! If it is possible, let this cup of suffering be taken away from me. Yet I want your will to be done, not mine."*

40 *Then he returned to the disciples and found them asleep. He said to Peter, "Couldn't you watch with me even one hour?* ***41*** *Keep watch and pray, so that you will not give in to temptation. For the spirit is willing, but the body is weak!"*

***42** Then Jesus left them a second time and prayed, "My Father! If this cup cannot be taken away unless I drink it, you will be done." **43** When he returned to them again, he found them sleeping, for they couldn't keep their eyes open.*

***44** So he went to pray a third time, saying the same things again"* **Matt 26:36-44**

If you had a spouse or best friend tell you they are dying in a few hours, and they want to take you somewhere one last time before they go, you would take that deeply seriously. Whatever place that person is taking you, has to be of great significance. You wouldn't spend your last living moments at a random place with no meaning; you would go somewhere that mattered.

Jesus doesn't take them to the temple. They don't go on a stroll to the synagogues. Jesus takes them to a garden.

Why a garden?

Because Jesus is about to redeem everything. Jesus is about to fix everything that has gone wrong in the world.

And how does he redeem it? He goes back to the place where it all went wrong.

A garden.

Remember Genesis chapters 2 and 3? Remember the story of Adam and Eve? They were placed in the garden, told to toil the land and care for it, told to not touch one specific tree.

What happens? Adam and Eve disobey, taking their will into their own hands and choose to not surrender to God. And their choice ruins humanity.

So what does Jesus do?

He goes back to the garden. As the last and perfect Adam. And he does the complete opposite of the first garden story. He does what the first Adam should have done.

Jesus redeems it. His nature is to be a restorer.

Adam disobey———Jesus obeys
Adam chooses his will———Jesus chooses God's will
Adam ruins humanity by a tree———-Jesus saves humanity on a tree
Adam gets us kicked out of paradise———Jesus welcomes us back into paradise
Adam put a chasm between us and God———-Jesus brought us back to God

Adam and Eve hide naked——-Jesus hung naked on the tree
Adam and Eve passed the fruit———Jesus passed communion
It was food that got us kicked out———it is food (communion with God) that welcomes us back in

Do you see it? The garden of gethsemane is the complete reversal of the first garden.

Therefore, of course Jesus went to a garden on his last night before the cross. It was an act of warfare. To take back what the enemy had stolen. It was an act of eternal restoration.

Furthermore not just the garden, but everything Jesus did in His life was a statement of redemption. Nothing he did was random. Every miracle, every sermon, every battle with the devil, every place his foot stepped, he was reclaiming ground.

You see, biblically, speaking Jesus is the fulfillment of everything in the Old Testament. The book of Hebrews talks about this in great length, that Jesus is greater. He is greater than Moses, greater than the angels, greater than the priesthood, greater than the temple. He is the fulfillment and redemption of everything we lost and ruined.

The cross and life of Jesus is shouting redemption. That's why Jesus yelled on the cross "it is finished" which in antiquity in the Greek language is a lawyer term that someone would yell when the gavel was being hit saying "its paid. It's fulfilled. It is finished"

Jesus is declaring on the cross: I paid it. It's over.

This garden that Jesus finds himself is no ordinary garden. It is called the garden of gethsemane for a reason: it is an olive press.

It is a place of crushing, a place of squeezing. It's where you would take olives and press them to get olive oil.

This is the place Jesus decides to take a walk to before the cross, not by accident, but as a prophetic statement because he is heading to the oil press: the cross.

Do you find yourself in gethsemane? It could be a physical gethsemane like Jesus, and you are currently enduring physical ailment in your body and it is squeezing the life out of you.

But I wonder how many of you are not in a literal gethsemane but in an emotional one? Your soul is being pressed and squeezed. You feel like life is squeezing, well, the life outta you.

Every person breathing on this earth will have what authors call “the dark night of the soul”. No one leaves this side of eternity unscathed; life touches us all.

Everyone will have their gethsemane moment. This is not dooms day preaching, or fire and brimstone is on the way. No, it’s just a fact of life.

Many times in a Christian’s life, prayers are offered to God that sound like this: Lord bring more into my life, I want new perspective, I want new power and authority, I want the new wine the Bible talks about...but we really have no idea what we are praying for.

We are praying for crushing. We are asking for squeezing. How do you get new oil? You press the olives.

You see, right now we live in a society that wants oil with no crushing.

We want the new without giving up the old.

We want the revelation without the trial.

We want the check without the work.

We want the title without the consistency.

We want a harvest without sowing.

Life for sure doesn't work that way. I don't believe God works that way.

Possibly, you are in a John the Baptist moment in your life, and you feel like Jesus isn't coming to get you out. You might feel like Jesus in the garden and life is crashing before your eyes.

Maybe instead of praying for escape, pray for revelation. Instead of asking why did this happen to me, ask who am I becoming because of this.

Or possibly some of you are on your way out of gethsemane right now. You feel yourself leaving this season and entering into a new one. Gethsemane has been the last few months or years for you, but you feel like you are leaving this season and heading into a new one.

I submit, you reflect on your way out of the garden. I have learned whatever you don't reflect on you are bound to repeat. So whether you are in the middle or on your way out. Stop, take a moment and reflect.

If the garden of Gethsemane is the place of crushing, the place where oil is squeezed, I'm not leaving the garden without my oil. If I have to go through it, I'm not walking out empty handed. If I have to endure this garden, I'm leaving with some oil. I'm leaving a better husband, I'm leaving a better father, I'm leaving a better friend, I'm leaving more like Christ. I refuse to leave empty handed, I want my oil!

What are you taking with you? What has changed in you during this season? Yes you have lost some things no doubt, but what have you gained?

I want you to learn from Jesus how to endure hardship. How to stand in the middle of a storm. Here in this story Jesus is teaching us how to handle the pressure moments of life. How to handle suffering.

This is why I believe this story of Jesus is one of the most profound scenes we see him in on this earth.

I want you to see four things from not only this text but from the overall life in the person of Jesus and how we can handle pain and suffering.

A GOD WHO BLEEDS

The way Christians interrupt and relate to pain is wildly different from every other religion or any spiritual guru. In the modern era we live in, it seems like most people who are not religious think the main religions are pretty much the same with a few diversions. Mormons, Buddhist, Christianity, Hindu, Muslim, it's pretty much all relative with a few name differences and some life-style practice differences.

When you begin to dive into those religions, you will find out very quickly, they are not similar at all. How we get forgiven, not the same at all. How we reach eternal bliss, not the same at all. The point of existence, not the same at all. How we relate to the divine, not the same at all.
But one of the major differences, especially between Christianity, Buddhism and Muslims, is the belief around pain and suffering.

Timothy Keller says it best in his work Walking Through Pain and Suffering —*"Christianity teaches that, contra fatalism, suffering is overwhelming; contra Buddhism, suffering is real; contra karma, suffering is often unfair; but contra secularism, suffering is meaningful. There is a purpose to it, and if faced rightly, it can drive us like a nail deep into the love of God and into more stability and spiritual power than you can imagine."*

I will repeat it again—Jesus and his way is the greatest answer to pain and suffering that humans possess.

So what makes Jesus and Christianity so different?

We serve a God who bleeds.

God is sovereign over suffering and yet God also made himself vulnerable and subject to suffering. This teaching is unique to the Christian faith among the major religions. There is a relationship between the sovereignty of God and the suffering of God, no other God in any other religion claims that relationship.

This God bleeds. This God cries. Yahweh decided to show himself vulnerable.

As Ronald Rittgers said "A God who is sovereign and a God who suffered, holding both of these together—as paradoxical as they seem at first—is crucial to grasping the unique Christian understanding of suffering"

Dan McCartney in his book *the meaning of Christian suffering* says *"the main reason that Christians insist that God can be trusted in the midst of suffering is that … God himself has firsthand experience of suffering"*

Those two quotes are incredibly profound and deeply true. One of the main reasons Jesus is trustworthy during times of sorrow and pain, is because he also experienced it.

Matt 26's account doesn't give the details, but the Luke account in chapter 22 has the details that Jesus was in so much agony, he sweated drops of blood. I have been stressed before, I have been anxious, but I have never sweat drops of blood.

Think about that. No seriously. Consider that the God we serve, decided to put skin and bone on, to become human, and suffer.

Of course Jesus knew, because he is Omniscient, that he was going to die a horrible death in a few days time. For Jesus did not come to earth just to live, he came to die. Jesus says in *John 15 "no man may take my life but i lay it down freely",* Jesus knew he was about to lay down his life.

What God would do that? What creator would choose to become like his creation, in his plan to save that very creation. And suffer at extreme levels to do so.

This is absolutely core to the Christian doctrine. This is a huge reason why you can trust Jesus with your pain, because he understands.

And by the way—talking about justice and fairness, what did Jesus do to die a sinner's death? Did Jesus deserve to be crucified while remaining completely innocent?

No. He was treated unfairly and unjustly. He lived in perfect obedience and perfectly in the center of God's will.

If you have experienced deeply sorrowful pain, that was unfair and so undeserved, and you are thinking 'no one understands me, no one gets it.'

Jesus does.

If you are a Christian, you don't serve a God who hides up in his ivory tower looking down upon the mere mortals of earth. God isn't some deity in his fortress, untouchable and unapproachable, no this God came down to earth. Jesus lived in the muck and mire of humanity, and experienced pain and suffering.

Have you ever had a best friend hurt you deeply? Jesus had one of his best friends sell him for money, to be murdered.

Have you ever felt like no one believed in you? Jesus was mocked, abandoned, and ridiculed, because most people didn't believe his claims, and then was killed for those claims. Jesus understands what it means to be deeply misunderstood.

Why does this matter so much? Because if God is all-knowing, never learning and growing in knowledge, why did he need to experience pain when he already understood it?

You know this—there is a great difference between understanding something based on intellect and experiencing it personally. God does not just understand pain, he experienced it.

The New Testament has a great deal to say how our suffering puts us in a position to share in Christ's sufferings. That through pain and suffering, we share in that glory together with Jesus. So something that happened to Jesus through suffering is now happening through you in suffering. There are some similarities there, but there is one big difference between our sufferings. You see, when Jesus suffered, he grew in human likeness, and when we suffer, we grow in Christlikeness. What I mean by that is Jesus could not grow in Christlikeness or grow in his Godness, for he is fully God, but he was not a human before his incarnation, so suffering grew his humanity. We on the other hand are fully human, and are now growing into our Christlikeness. Suffering forms our Christlikeness unlike any other experience in our life.

If Jesus, the son of God, didn't make it through this life on earth without pain and suffering, why do we think we will?

St Augustine declares, *"God had one son on earth without sin, but never one without suffering."*

A DIFFERENT KIND OF KING

A core doctrine of Christianity is the kingship of Jesus. We believe that Jesus was not just a prophet, not just a teacher, not just a moral leader and spiritual thinker. No, we believe He is King.

When you think of the ancient civilization when Jesus walked the earth some 2,000 years ago, all were quite familiar with kings and queens, royalty, Caesars, because all that kind of stuff was their daily reality.

When Kings and Caesars would go to and from war, after they were victorious and when they entered a town, there was a decorum. The entire town would come out, cheer and celebrate, throwing their garments on the floor, and usually yell "All hail Caesar." When kings and queens would have children, the entire city would be notified and there would be the most prestigious banquets and parties.

But not King Jesus. He is not like the other kings.

Think about the birth of Jesus. He is not born in a palace, with the royal entourage surrounding him. He was born in obscurity. He was born in a dirty stable.

Think about his arrival statement riding into Jerusalem the week he would be crucified. He rode in on a donkey.

Not a chariot with war horses. Not this king, he rides in humbly.

Why would Jesus do this? Why would Jesus live this kind of life? Because Jesus came to be a king unlike the world had ever seen. He came as the humble King.

If Jesus came to earth, floated through life, never experienced pain, sadness, or loss, and then just ascended back up into heaven: how could we trust that person when we are suffering? Well you couldn't. How could we relate to that person? We wouldn't be able to; there would be a massive gap emotionally and mentally, living a completely different human experience.

"So then, since we have a great High Priest who has entered heaven, Jesus the Son of God, let us hold firmly to what we believe. This High Priest of ours understands our weaknesses, for he faced all of the same testings we do, yet he did not sin. So let us come boldly to the throne of our gracious God. There we will receive his mercy, and we will find grace to help us when we need it most ***Hebrews 4: 14-16***

The reason why we can come so boldly to the throne room with our prayer and worship is because our high priest Jesus understands us and knows our weakness. We don't approach the throne room because we are pure enough to do so, or because we have done so much good we feel the right to. We approach the throne boldly because of the one who sits on it, not because of the one who is approaching it.

The doctrine of Jesus' suffering, I believe, is one of the important doctrines we must not let go. It must not fade into the background of literature and intellect. It must stay at the forefront of Christians' minds and conversations.

We serve a God who bleeds.

Right now as I write this in 2025, one of the most popular Christian songs is called "Son of sSuffering" here are a few of the lyrics

And in the end, the proof is in Your wounds
Yes, in the end, the proof is in Your wounds
Blood and tears
How can it be?
There's a God who weeps
There's a God who bleeds
Oh, praise the One
Who would reach for me
Hallelujah to the Son of suffering

Friends, let this be our anthem.

This is the gospel. This is our King.

King Jesus' birth was different, but so was his death.

Did you see the phrase in the passage we looked at "*My Father! If it is possible, let this cup of suffering be taken away from me".* What an interesting phrase for Jesus to pray to God the father. Let this cup be taken? What cup?

Let me help you fill in the historical gaps.

In ancient times of the Roman Empire, when a King would conquer another land, if the conquest ended in victory, something very important happened on their way home. After defeating another land and people, they would capture the other nation's King or Caesar, and high ranking officers. They would try and not kill them during battle, because once the war was over, they would bring them back to the kingdom, defeated and ashamed. They wanted to publicly shame them.

The Roman Empire would have a procession into the kingdom, with all the warriors coming home from battle and the defeated foe in the back of the line, ashamed. When they got back to the Roman kingdom, they would make a line of the king or highest ranking officer to the lowest ranking officers in front of the town. They would put a cup of poison into the hand of the highest ranking officer first.

The King had a choice. Drink the entire cup of poison, killing himself, but saving the rest of the officers, or he could choose to pass the cup to the next person in line. If every person in the line passed the cup, the entire line would be killed.

So therefore, the first person in line, the king, had a choice to make. Drink it or pass it.

So you see, Jesus is using this same language, as a King. Asking his father, if anyone else can drink this cup but me, let me please pass it, but if I must, I will drink it. You know how the story ends, Jesus drank the cup. Our king drank the cup of death, so that we now will never have to.

But what was the cup a representation of? Eternal Death, not temporal suffering. Jesus did not take the cup of suffering so that every person who puts their trust in him would never taste suffering. No, it was that every person who puts their trust in him would never taste death but everlasting life.

Let us be reminded the most important thing Jesus saved us from is not pain and suffering, it is sin and death. Jesus never promised earthly safety, but He did promise heavenly assurance. He doesn't offer a safe journey, but a safe destination.

So when the Roman Empire crucified Jesus, they thought he was being publicly shamed. But in reality, Jesus was publicly shaming death, sin, and the forces of hell. As the saying goes, the joke was on them. Jesus won, death lost.

RELATIONAL WISDOM

My mom was born and raised in Melbourne Australia and moved to America in the 70s with her family, then married my dad during her college years. My dad's side of the family is from the Azore Islands in Portugal and moved to New York in the 1940s and then eventually migrated over to California and settled there.

So both sides of my family are immigrants to America, people who left everything behind, including family, to pursue a new life in this nation.

This is important to point out because I wasn't raised with family around. My mom's family stayed in Australia and my dad wasn't too close with his family or siblings later in life. I wasn't raised with family vacations with all the cousins, in laws, and big holiday celebrations.

I was raised to make friends and have them become family. From the age of 4 to 23 we went on summer vacation with the same five families. They became my uncles, aunts, and cousins. They were really the only extended family I had.

Because of this, friendships are of the utmost importance to me. They are the life in my veins and the air in my lungs. To this day my friends in my life are my family; they are the most important possessions I have. I don't know how to have casual friends very well, I only know how to live in deep interwoven communities.

I would submit that the health of your life is determined by the health of your relationships. You have thrived in life while being surrounded by broken relationships. Our relationships not only set the course of our life they also set the tone of our life.

Why do I share this? Because this is also modeled by Jesus. He wasn't some Lone Ranger, doing life completely alone as the hero of the cosmos, floating through life untouchable and unreachable.

Jesus himself lived in deep relationships with his disciples, especially the 12 that he did ministry with for 3 1/2 years. But you must catch this, he didn't just do ministry with those 12 dudes, he did life with them. He was deeply relational. If Jesus wasn't a Lone Ranger, neither should you be.

Back to our scene with Jesus in the garden. He has shown us that we serve a God who bleeds and knows what it means to experience pain. Then Jesus does something really interesting while experiencing this pain, he shows us how to handle relationships during painful moments in our life.

"Then Jesus went with them to the olive grove called Gethsemane, and he said, "Sit here while I go over there to pray." ***37*** *He took Peter and Zebedee's two sons, James and John, and he became anguished and distressed.* ***38*** *He told them, "My soul is crushed with grief to the point of death. Stay here and keep watch with me."* ***Matt 26:36-44***

Did you see what Jesus just did?

To his 11 closest friends in his life here on earth, he tells them to sit down and wait while he goes and prays. Then he tells Peter, James and John to come with him. He doesn't tell the 11 all the information, only his three best friends.

Wait? That seems unfair, exclusive, and kinda rude. To tell his other friends to sit and wait while he invites the three to go where the others can't.

Jesus is not doing any of those things, he is showing us relationship wisdom in times of suffering. If Jesus is allowed to have different levels of friends and different circles of intimacy with his friends, so are you.

It's not unloving or exclusive; it's wisdom.

NOT EVERYONE NEEDS TO KNOW

Hopefully during times of pain and suffering, a lot of your friends will want to come to your aid and ask you how you are doing, what you need, and if you want to talk about it. However, what some of these friends are wanting is for you to pour your heart out, tell them everything, and if you don't, you are being a "fake friend" or not being transparent enough for them. If you withhold information or details from them, they feel like you're being secretive.

During the season of excruciating pain I described earlier in this book, so many people would ask me "how are you doing?" and I would say fine, and they would reply back, "no how are you *really* doing?" And I would say back again, "it's a really hard season but I'm okay." I always felt bad about it, like I was lying and not being totally truthful to people that wanted to help. But I also simultaneously felt like I couldn't share the state of my soul with certain people. I felt trapped. Until Jesus showed me a better way in this Garden story.

Do you see the order in which this story is told? First Jesus says to the group, "you guys sit here," and then he takes his three best friends for a little walk, and THEN he says "My soul is crushed with grief to the point of death. Stay here and keep watch with me." He does not say those words to the entire group, he waits until he is alone with his closer friends to share that information.

Especially when it comes to communities of faith and friendship within churches, you can feel like you need to treat every relationship equal and to not have favorites. That is just not true. If Jesus is allowed to be selective with who he gives information to, so am I.

Because the truth is, some people just can't handle all the details. Not every person deserves to know the state of your soul. Your pain is not in safe hands with every friend you have.

Peter, James and John were Jesus' best friends. Throughout the gospels you will notice that Jesus takes them places he doesn't take the others, he tells them things he doesn't tell the others, they see miracles the others don't see.

I think sometimes as a Christian and in church circles, there can be the notion that you aren't allowed to have best friends, or different levels or relationships; you need to love everyone equally. That is just not true, and it's not seen in the life of Jesus.

There is a difference between being fake and being guarded. I'm not claiming we should be fake to everyone, to lie and not really share how we are doing to those in our communities and life. There is a way to be honest, share enough that needs to be said, while remaining guarded. Like I mentioned above. I would say, "it's a really hard season, but I'm okay." I call this generic honesty.

In the text, Jesus is giving every one of his followers the permission and the wisdom to have different levels of friendships that tell different parts of your life, too.

It's called wisdom. There is a big difference between being clicky and having a clique. Being clicky is being really exclusive and rude. But the fact is, there are just some people you clique with, more than others, and that's called relational wisdom.

So right about now you are probably asking the million dollar question, how can I know who is in what circle? How can I know who is in the three and who is in the nine?

Great question. Let's look at another story really fast. Because Matthew 26 is not the only intimate moment these three have with Jesus that the other nine don't. There is another fascinating story a few chapters earlier in Matthew.

"After six days Jesus took with him Peter, James and John the brother of James, and led them up a high mountain by themselves. ***2*** *There he was transfigured before them. His face shone like the sun, and his clothes became as white as the light.* ***3*** *Just then there appeared before them Moses and Elijah, talking with Jesus" Matthew 17:1-3*

This is an absolutely wild story when you read the rest of it. We won't get into the theological significance right now, but I do want you to see something.

Who is there? Peter. James. John. The same three again are in a situation and moment that the other nine are not invited into.

Again in this story Jesus is showing the level of friendships and dynamics of having best friends.
So to briefly answer your question, I would like to offer a couple thoughts.

First, you can't force this type of friendship. They are God-breathed and made over time. Right now would be a bad and awkward choice to randomly text a few friends and say "hey do you want to be my Peter James and John?" Don't do it.

You don't really pick relationships like this. They are just formed over time, through seasons, through the ups and the downs. It's the people God knits your heart with theirs. There are some friends you will have for a long time, amazing people in your life, but they just don't grow to this level of intimacy. For whatever reasons, they just don't. But there are some people that God just draws together, and you wake up one day noticing their significance in your life.

Second, these relationships come from those who can see your face shine and your soul bleed. Do you see what Peter James and John get to see that no one else does in the life of Jesus? The mountain top of his face shining like the sun and the valley of Gethsemane where his soul was crushed.

Not everyone can handle both of those moments. Some people only like the mountain tops, the paydays and the blessings, but they disappear during the valleys. Other people only like the valleys, they are drawn to pain, they are drawn to the down and out moments of life, but they can't handle the mountain tops. They think it's fake and too earthly; they are weirdly allergic to joy. The mountain tops aren't "deep enough" for them and the valley is where real life happens.

We need people who can do what the Apostle Paul says in Romans *"rejoice with those who rejoice and weep with those who weep."*. The Peter, James and John friends are those that can see both seasons of your life.

So what are some early and elementary ways to start making these types of friends? It's actually pretty simple. Hard to do, but simple to understand.

MAKING FRIENDS

There is a fascinating book that was written by a hospice nurse named Bronnie Ware who would spend the last hours of people's lives, by their side, preparing them for death. Sometimes in situations when their families couldn't be in the room, she would walk people into eternity. A job many of us could not stomach. She did it for years, and at the end of her time in this field, she wrote a book about it called *"The top five regrets of the dying"*

While spending many hours with these people preparing them for death, she would of course get to know them very well, answering and asking a lot of life's biggest questions, deeply assessing life's meaning.

She writes in her book that the number #1 regret of the dying is, "I wish I had stayed in touch with my friends"

She writes *"Often the patients would not truly realize the full benefits of old friends until their dying weeks and it was not always possible to track them down. Many had become so caught up in their own lives that they had let golden friendships slip by over the years. There were many deep regrets about not giving friendships the time and effort that they deserved. Everyone misses their friends when they are dying. They would say "my priorities in life got disordered."*

That's right. At the end of our lives people are thinking about their relationships. Not their assets or their 401k, but their friends.

Dr Curt Thompson adds to the conversation "*we are all born into the world looking for someone looking for us"*

So if these two are correct, and I believe they are, at the beginning and the end of our lives, we are looking for people.

We are living in a cultural moment that many sociologists have named "crowded loneliness." We are all looking for friendships and life partners, but apparently we can't seem to find them?

We are the most connected generation to ever live, and we're not even close. With the internet and social media, we are connected to more people than we know what to do with. Yet we are also the most lonely and fragmented generation to ever live.

How does that work? How can we have apps like facebook and instagram at our fingertips yet feel so alone? You would think these devices would fix it, but yet it's making it worse.
Sociologist Robert Bellah said, "We are the generation that watches *Friends* without having them. We don't need more friends, we need deeper ones."

PRIORITY

Many psychologists have written about how our current generation has a hard time committing. We like to keep our options open, we like to be free away from our calendar, and see where the wind takes us. Specifically with people, we are having a hard time living in deep commitment with other people.

And sometimes I believe one of the reasons we are having a hard time having deep friendships is because we don't make it a priority. Our lives are too busy for real community.

We have our career to build, our passports to fill up, our schooling to finish, and our money to spend. We just don't make people a priority anymore. Our priorities have gotten disordered. We have forgotten the riches of life are people, not things.

If we aren't careful we are going to wake up in our old age, look around at tables and find them empty. Our back accounts will be full, but our hearts will be empty. Our contact lists will be full of business connections, but our dinner tables will be empty.

What is the state of your current relationships? Do you have deep intimate friends?

And please don't tell me you have a lot of Linkedin friends and followers on Instagram. Those friends are assets and networking opportunities. I don't mean how many likes you get on a photo, or how many work colleagues like you.

I mean, friends that are like family.

Are you making the people in your life priority? I know this is shocking to you, especially if you are an American, but maybe giving your business less attention and your relationships more is what your heart is missing. Maybe your heart isn't missing more money, more accolades, and a new corner office, but deeper relationships. Our western world and specifically America is great at breeding individualistic and self-centered humans. Life is all about you, for you and by you. You are number 1, follow your heart and secure the bag. Come fulfill the American dream.

Well, is it working? Is the American dream fulfilling your deepest longings in your heart? I'd venture to say, not quite.

If we are going to live what the Scriptures offer, we must make people the priority.

Author and historian, Dr Joseph Hellerman in his brilliant book *When the church was a family* says, "*Spiritual formation occurs primarily in the context of community. People who remain connected with their brothers and sisters in the local church almost invariably grow in self-understanding, and they mature in their ability to relate in healthy ways to God and to their fellow human beings. This is especially the case for those courageous Christians who stick it out through the often messy process of interpersonal discord and conflict resolution. Long-term interpersonal relationships are the crucible of genuine progress in the Christian life. People who stay grow. People who leave do not grow. We all know people who are consumed with spiritual wanderlust. But we never get to know them very well because they cannot seem to stay put. They move along from church to church, ever searching for a congregation that will better satisfy their felt needs. Like trees repeatedly transplanted from soil to soil, these spiritual nomads fail to put down roots and seldom experience lasting and fruitful growth in their Christian lives."*

The relationships that Hellerman speaks of take time, years and years; they don't come overnight. This type of community is cultivated not dreamt. You don't just wake up one morning with this kind of community surrounding you, it is cultivated day after day.

They don't come easy either. You have to fight for a community that like. Fighting through getting let down, talking through jokes that weren't funny and cut you to pieces, working out the offenses of life. This is the real stuff, this is the heart of real friendship.

Why do we have to fight so hard to make people a priority? We know that relationships are important, so why don't we just make it happen?

Because our modern world is no longer in favor of deep intimate communities.

Sebastian Junger in his book *Tribe*, an award winning journalist says it perfectly, *"A person living in a modern city or a suburb can, for the first time in history, go through an entire day—or an entire life—mostly encountering complete strangers. They can be surrounded by others and yet feel deeply, dangerously alone. We can go through an entire day without encountering anyone, and many people are opting for this. We can shop and gather information online, at the touch of a button. In either case, unless we now prioritize connecting with people in meaningful ways, the structure of our modern society is designed for disconnection. It leads us to actually believe we can live without others."*

Did you see it? "Modern society is designed for disconnection."

Fascinating.

That is deeply profound and absolutely accurate. Our current society is designed for you to not need people, and in some ways not even want them. You just need you and Siri. And you and I both know in the center of our soul, that's a lie. This is not working, it's actually ruining our society at its very core.

You see, one of the main things that times of pain and suffering can do in our life is deeply affect our relationships, in a negative way. It can cause great tension, frustration, division, and we can lose the very relationships at the time we need them more than ever.

We must prioritize the people closest to us during these seasons of heartache and loss, not run away.

One of the positive things that pain does, it can reorder and prioritize friendships. Meaning, it can bring those closer to you that you need during this time, and those who you don't, specifically need to take a step back for the moment. Different seasons demand different friendships. Raising children, you need certain advice. Buying a new business requires different input. The same with pain and suffering, during these moments there are certain relationships you need to greatly lean into.

But this does not happen accidentally; it is chosen, it is prioritized. Jesus prioritized Peter, James, and John being with him. They didn't ask Jesus to be there, Jesus asked them. He made sure he wasn't alone during the darkest moment of his life thus far.

Maybe right now you are reading this book, and pain has dragged you away into the cave of isolation. I beg you, fight for community. Fight to make it a priority.

Pain has already stolen from you enough, don't let it steal anymore. Don't let it steal another second.

VULNERABILITY

Who knows you? I mean the real you, not the social media you, or the you that work friends who get 40 hours a week with and who know your lunch order.

Do you have people in your life that know the real you? The good and the bad, the broken sides of you and the glorious sides of you? A few of you read a few pages ago when I talked about not everyone needs to know, and something in you yelled "Yes! See i knew it, people need to leave me alone and get out of my business"

I said not *everyone* needs to know, I did not say *no one* needs to know.

I believe another major reason why we can't find real friends is because we either don't want to be vulnerable or we don't know how to.

We live in the filter, perfect, post only your highlights moment. There is no room for scars or failures. The fear of being vulnerable is very real because chances are you will either be cancelled or lose those friends.

It will change your human existence. If you can find friends that you can show your shadows to, the dark part of your soul, they will not only stick around but be there to help you grow and develop.

In order for us to pursue the biblical idea of *koinonia*, which is a Greek word painting a picture of the deepest and most intimate relationships we can have, we must learn how to be vulnerable and give space to people to be vulnerable with us.

I encourage you to commit to these two simple ideas: prioritize friendships and be vulnerable with them.

This profound text in Matthew 26, Jesus is showing us how to do friendship. How to live in real time in an interwoven connection with others.

If Jesus needed real friends during his darkest moment, so did you. Jesus didn't act like a superhero not needing anyone because he was strong enough to handle it himself. No, Jesus is showing us how to live life.

Now you are probably thinking right about now, this sounds risky. This sounds like it could get really messy. Oh yes, incredibly messy and very difficult. But absolutely worth it.

CS Lewis speaks to this idea in *Four Loves, "To love at all is to be vulnerable. Love anything and your heart will certainly be wrung and possibly broken. If you want to make sure of keeping it intact, you must give your heart to no one, not even an animal. Wrap it carefully around with hobbies and little luxuries, avoid all entanglements. Lock it safe up in the casket or coffin of your selfishness. But in that casket—safe, dark, motionless, airless; your heart will change. It will not be broken; it will become unbreakable, impenetrable, irredeemable."*

This is the idea the Apostle Paul was speaking of when he wrote in Galatians chapter 6, "bear one another burdens." He is not just speaking of the burdens of life, like helping pick up each other's kids from school, helping with some bills, and helping load the moving truck. Yes, those burdens, but more than that, the burdens of our sins and our souls, those kinds of burdens.

As we wrap up this section, let's go back to a line in Matt 26:38, *"He told them, "My soul is crushed with grief to the point of death. Stay here and keep watch with me."*

Jesus wasn't just aware of his crushed soul, he tells his friends about it, and then asks them to come and sit with him.

Look at how normal this is. The son of God, the perfect and holy one, is going through a deep dark moment in his life, and he just wants his friends to come sit with him. He doesn't want to be alone at this moment.

Catch this, Jesus didn't want for them to assume it, he didn't wait for them to "be good friends to him," he vocalized it, he told his friends what he needed.

Jesus doesn't just tell himself and tell God, he tells his friends about the state of his soul.

Who in your life are you able to share the state of soul with? Not just when your soul is flourishing, those friends are easy to find, but when your soul is crushed and in despair.

If the son of God needed friends, so do you.

If the son of God needed friends to come and sit with him in his pain, so do you.

If the son of God needed to vocalize the state of his soul, so do you.

I would greatly challenge you to set this book aside for a few moments. This might be a divinely important time for you to consider the state of your relationships, friendship, and those who fill your life and your dinner table.

Maybe ask a few of these questions:

- who am I deeply committed to?
- who is deeply committed to me?

- who truly knows me?
- are there any relationships i am taking for granted?
- who would I go to during life's darkest moments?

Oftentimes during times of pain and suffering, we can shut down, put on the smile, grit our teeth and get through it.

When I was younger I thought that vulnerability was like giving people ammo, giving them bullets to later shoot me with. Being vulnerable was not a safe thing to do, and showing the dark sides of you was not a good idea; that's how you get in trouble, that's how you lose friends. I was totally unaware that it was the complete opposite. Being vulnerable is how you gain the right friends, and lose the wrong ones.

I don't know about you, but I was drawn to think that vulnerability was weakness. I didn't want to show my pain, let alone talk about it. I honestly used to believe that being vulnerable would only make things worse, not better"

I missed out on so many good moments in my friendships and my church community, because I was fearful.

It can be embarrassing, it can feel like people will treat you like a project, or a broken person needing to be fixed.

Being vulnerable is difficult and takes great courage and trust in those standing in front of you.

Deep within, I know this and so do you: we have to do it, there is no other option. We must fight against the pull to retreat, to hide, to shut down.

We must have the friends surrounding our dinner tables to weep with, to show our shadows to, to open up the corridors of our soul knowing they won't run for the door.

Having a community to be vulnerable with during the loss, anger, disappointment, is like a soothing oil to your soul.

EMOTIONAL HONESTY

While my dad was fighting cancer I was 25 years old, our first son was 6 months old, and we had been married just for 3 years. I didn't know how to handle it. Looking back, I know I didn't handle it well emotionally. I just didn't know what to do with my emotions or my questions. Sure, I did the best I could with a young baby and a new marriage, and I used the tools I had. But emotionally, I didn't know how to process it. I didn't know how to communicate with my wife or friends. So I didn't. I smiled and kept moving forward. I shoved everything as far down as it could go.

As I have mentioned, my favorite author and church father was St. Augustine from the 4th century. He stands out for multiple reasons, but mainly I love how he talks to God. How he shows his raw emotions, his anger, his questions about God, and his ways. He is fully himself before God. St Augustine wrote in Confessions, *"How can you draw close to God when you are far from your own self? Grant me, Oh Lord, that I may know myself so that I might know you."*

I didn't know who I was during that time. I was far away from myself and my true emotions, because I truly thought I was being a good Christian and a good leader by ignoring all emotions. Especially the so-called bad ones, like anger and resentment.

I answered every question with "I'm good! We will make it through! Today was hard, but God is good!"

And sure, all of those answers were true, God is good and we did make it through, but I didn't mean any of those answers. They weren't authentic or from my heart, they weren't what I wanted to say or how I felt.

I didn't know then what I know now: God honors and leans into, not away from, those who are emotionally honest to themselves and to God.

Look at the book of Psalms and God's relationship to King David. David says things to God I would be scared to utter in a prayer. David asks things of God I didn't know I was allowed to voice.

And yet David is a man after God's own heart. Jesus himself comes through the line of David and sits on the throne of David.

HOW TO BE HUMAN

This is one of my favorite scenes in the life of Jesus, because he is showing us how to be human. One of the most shocking aspects of this story for me is that Jesus is not only in tune with his emotions but he expresses them.

To further unpack this point, when Jesus says to Peter James and John, "my soul is crushed, even to the point of death," Jesus is talking about deep seated emotions. That word crushed or sorrowful in the Greek language is very descriptive of emotions as deep as depression, sadness, or deep sorrow. Jesus is not having a bad day, he isn't just a little emotional or kinda annoyed, he is crushed. His heart and soul hurt. Interestingly enough the term "sick to death" came from these words. Other gospel writers say that he began to sweat blood. I have been anguished, in pain, and very upset before, but I have never sweat blood.

Jesus is showing the fullness of his humanity at this moment.

And you must catch this Jesus is showing his best friends his raw emotions, and he is honest about them.

Jesus doesn't get in the garden and say, "Praise the Lord, God is good, everything is okay, I'm totally fine,

God is on the throne!" He doesn't give his best friends all the Christian jargon and catchy church phrases.

Why do we feel like being emotionally honest is turning our back on God? Why do we give people funny answers when they ask us how we are doing and everything in us wants to say, "I'm not doing well, I feel like God is distant and not answering my prayers, and I really feel like quitting and giving up."

If you said that to someone in the church parking lot after service, they would think you just denied Jesus and you are on your way to the pit of fire. I think sometimes when we become a Christian, people think we stop being human. It's like we have divorced our humanity from our Christianity.

So when people ask us how we are doing, we give a half true answer and say something around "I'm doing okay, life is hard right now, but God is good!" and shove our real emotions as far down as they can go. Because that's what good Christian men and women do! Right.....?

No friends, Jesus doesn't show us that. He shows us how to be fully human with emotional honesty while being fully faithful to God.

Notice who Jesus is being emotionally vulnerable with: himself and his friends.

If you aren't emotionally in tune with yourself, and sifting through the corridors of your heart and soul, how can you be honest with your closest friends?

Do you know the state of your soul right now? The state of your emotions? Have you taken any time lately to literally sit down and be in silence, and let the depth of your soul begin to rise to the surface. I think sometimes for many of us, we stay so busy and active so we don't have to talk to ourselves. We also have music on, the Netflix show going, because we know if our life gets quiet our soul gets loud.

I challenge you to pray this bold prayer of King David

Ps 139:23-24 "Search me, O God, and know my heart; test me and know my anxious thoughts. 24 Point out anything in me that offends you, and lead me along the path of everlasting life"

King David is asking God "show me, me." Point out and show me the areas of myself I do not see. The parts of me that are offensive or anxious. We don't pray things like this, do we? We don't want God to search us and know us, and we especially don't want God to test us.

Why?

Because we know what's inside. We know what lurks beneath the surface.

In this garden, in this place of deep pain, Jesus is liberating the human heart to be human.

EMOTIONS AND SPIRITUALITY

There has been a weird stigma in church history with the scriptures, God, and therapy. If you were raised in the church in the 80's and 90's in certain circles, and you told someone that you were going to counseling or were seeing a therapist, the typical response would be a large gasp of shock. Then the person would proceed with something like, you not trusting in God enough and not praying hard enough.

But if I told that same person I went to the dentist last week to get my tooth fixed, they wouldn't think anything of it. They would never say that was a lack of faith.

Why? Why is it not a lack of faith to go get my tooth fixed but it's a lack of faith to get my soul and emotions fixed?

Therapy was viewed as weak, anti-faith, and not what true Christian's should be doing. They would tell a person battling depression to just pray harder, someone riddled with anxiety to just read the scriptures out loud, and to someone experiencing deep loss and sadness to find the joy of the Lord in their valley.

I don't understand pastorally or theologically how this crept into the church, considering all of the wisdom literature books in the Bible: proverbs, psalms, Ecclesiastes, job, Song of Solomon. I mean, talk about a range of emotions, deep seated anger, depression, anxiety, pain and suffering, you name it. Those 5 books show the gambit of the human experience on this earth. Those 5 books made it in the canon of scripture for the universal church--past, present and future--to read and mediate upon, and yet there was a church era where we acted like they didn't.

Now maybe some of you reading this are shaking your head and having a really hard time understanding that what I just said could even be possibly true; there is no way certain church circles treated people's emotions like that.

And others of you know exactly what I'm talking about and have experienced it first hand.
Unfortunately, this is a very real side of church history, at least in America, that happened over the last few decades. But thankfully the tides have turned greatly

over the last 15 years, and mental health is a massive narrative in our current society.

God cares deeply about the state of your soul and emotional well being.

It is a foolish notion to believe that it is possible to be spiritually thriving and emotionally devastated. That's like saying you are dying of cancer and you are in perfect health. These are not compatible statements. It is the same with the health of your inner and outer world. To be thriving on the outside and dying on the inside is not God's desire or design for your life.

Spiritual health+Emotional health=Godly health

3 John 3:2 "Beloved, I pray that all may go well with you and that you may be in good health, as it goes well with your soul"

The state of our soul and emotions is a big deal to God. The word soul is used 828 times in the bible, and over 700 of those times are in the Old Testament.

Just for a bit of review because it was many pages ago that I introduced this word, the Hebrew word soul is the word Neseph which has two meanings: it can mean the breath of a living person or throat and neck.

Throat and neck? And the breath of a living person? How could it mean two seemingly opposite things? Remember, we talked about that because they believed that just like whatever comes in and out of your throat is a matter of life and death (food and water), so it is a matter of life and death what comes in and out of your soul.

To the Jewish mind, you didn't have a soul, you are a soul. Your body is not the realest thing about you, your soul is.

The state of the human heart,the soul, the inner world, is a core theme of the scripture. It is not a random blip on the screen, it's a motif that runs all through all 66 books. Your inner world greatly matters to God.

WE HAVE UNHEALTHY RELATIONSHIP WITH OUR SOUL

Maybe you are reading this and you are in therapy, you are healthy, thriving, and you are in deep connection with your soul, past trauma, and family of origin. Congratulations, and God bless you. But for the rest of us that are still wading through the muck and mire of our emotions, we tend to have an unhealthy relationship with our soul.

I am no psychologist nor a therapist, but I have been in my fair share of counseling sessions and have read enough to have an elementary grasp on a few ideas. And in my opinion, there are typically two ways that we have an unhealthy relationship with our soul and emotions.

We shove them and ignore them

Or

We live in them constantly.

Let's address each one, just for a quick second. This isn't a counseling book, nor do I have the appropriate letters behind my last name to write in-depth, so let me just share a few basic thoughts.

IGNORING THEM

Have you ever seen that 7-year old kid at the pool party, who has the huge beach ball between his legs trying to shove it under water, and it's just not happening? It shoots up from the water every time he tries and he just shoves it down farther.

That's what we look like emotionally at times. We are just shoving, shoving, shoving, trying to hide all the deep emotions under the surface as much as we can. You might be able to for a little while, but emotional gravity will win every time. It will come shooting up, until we realize we can't shove our emotions like a beach ball for too long.

I have much to say about this end because this is me. I shove emotions. I don't like addressing them, and I would rather just keep trucking ahead believing everything will be fine.

As I mentioned earlier when my dad was fighting cancer, I just didn't know what to do. I didn't know what I felt or how to express what I felt, and I got really, really good with that beach ball. I could ignore or hide a good portion of my emotions.

For a while. Then they all came rushing like a flood a few months later.

I think people that shove and ignore their emotions typically just don't know how to handle them, so they hide them. We are scared to express things that are so deep and intimate to us. We have a hard time using words to express what we feel in the depth of our being.

To all those who identify with this experience: Don't suppress your emotions, surrender them. What I mean by that is to surrender them to God through prayer in real time, with real emotion and honesty. Live in them, sit in them, wrestle with yourself.

How do you practically surrender? Here are two simple thoughts:

One, Read the psalms out loud, memorize them, meditate upon them. Use King David and the Psalms as your road map. Let me talk to every man reading this just for a moment. Having emotions and sharing those emotions is not feminine or weak, it is truly a sign of strength. Think of King David. This man was a warrior, a battle-tested man's man. His life would put gladiator and braveheart to shame. And yet, he also writes these psalms with deep, deep-seated emotions, honesty and a tenderness of heart. Being a real man is knowing when to be a lion and when to be a lamb. The most important way to surrender your emotions is through prayer in total honesty.

Two, go to a great counselor, not just anyone, because a bad counselor can do great damage. But with this great counselor, begin sifting through your family of origin, your upbringing, past experiences, and the things that make you, you. I have no idea why there is a weird stigma in the church community when people go to counseling. If you tell a christian you are going to therapy, it can be looked at like a lack of faith or trust in

God. “well isn’t that what prayer is for? Why don’t you just pray more about?”

Of course I believe in the power of prayer, and yes, God is the wonderful counselor, I get it. But isn’t there an entire book in the bible called proverbs, and chapter after chapter that book tells us to get counsel, pursue wisdom, get advice and direction from others. Going to the dentist for a broken tooth is not a lack of faith, going to therapy for a broken soul is also not a lack of faith.

When I started going to counseling, as a pastor, this is what I realized: the counselor’s job is to reveal what is broken, open my eyes to blind spots, then the Holy Spirit heals what is revealed. From a christian standpoint, i dont believe counseling actually heals us, it reveals what God needs to heal. I would walk out of counseling sessions, and surrender my thoughts and emotions to the Lord.

So this is why you need both. You need God’s word to wash over you, heal you, change you, and you need help to see those blind spots and wounds.

One of the major things I learned from the seasons of me shoving all emotions to the abyss of my soul: Unprocessed pain is doing unknown damage.

That's right. There is probably some floating dysfunction in your world and your relationships. It's probably subtle and not always detectable. But it's causing pain and damage you might not even notice yet, and it's stemming from unprocessed pain.

For example: for those of you who were not raised in church, there is a very real unsaid persona of the pastors' families and their children. The pastor's kids aren't usually treated like everyone else, and they are not allowed to fail or not be perfect. If a pastor's kid does something most other kids do, it is not viewed that way. It is, "I can't believe the pastor's son would do something like that." A child's actions can tarnish the view of the whole home. So therefore that trained me to not share anything going on in my life. Through middle school and high school I would never ever tell a youth pastor or staff member what was truly going on, because in my mind honesty wasn't really an option. So I became wildly independent, didn't need anything from anyone, and learned how to self regulate my emotions and processed with myself. I thought this was a strength and gift.

Until I went to counseling.

I soon found out that through that kind of childhood, it taught me not to trust people, it taught me to shove and hide my emotions, to not be honest with people, and avoid vulnerability.

I had no idea I was doing this under the guise of a "strength."

This emotional ideal for me transferred over into my marriage and my friendships. And as you would imagine, began to cause some damage that I was unaware of until my counselor began to show me.

Unknown damage causing unknown pain.

But this took time, and I was not fond of counseling in the beginning.

The first time my wife and I ever went to counseling together, on the way there I said one of the stupidest things to her. I said "This is going to be really good for you. I'm glad you are going to be able to express all your pain and trauma."

Yes. That's real. I actually said that.

Because I actually believed I didn't need counseling. I had nothing to talk though. I had no pain or trauma. Life had been hard for sure, but whose life wasn't? I was fine.

After about 30 min of Julia talking to our counselor, I was still thinking, "Wow this is so good for her. I'm so thankful."

Then the counselor turned and looked at me and said, "What about you, Andrew, what would you like to talk about?".

And I legit said, "Oh nothing, I'm here to support her."

She said in the most soft and kind tone, "Oh, I don't think so."

So I began to answer her questions, and about three hours later, my whole world had been ripped apart. I had no idea the pain hiding my heart, and I wasn't aware of the resentment lurking in my soul. There was unknown pain, and for the first time I realized all of the pain it was causing to those around me. I didn't see it, I wasn't aware of it. But just because you don't see it, doesn't mean it's not wreaking havoc in your mind and your relationships.

Unprocessed pain is doing unknown damage.

I am encouraging every one of you reading this who lean toward shoving, hiding, and ignoring your emotions, to find space and time to start unraveling your inner world.

LIVING IN THEM

The other end of our unhealthy relationship to our soul and emotions is the complete opposite. We don't shove, hide or ignore them, we fully live in them to the highest extent.

People on this end have zero trouble communicating how they feel and what they feel. They are usually completely in tune with their emotions, but their emotions typically have control of them and their decisions. They don't have control of their emotions, their emotions have control over them.

Typically what can happen with this type of response is your life can have really high highs and really low lows. Life is happening to you, and you are merely responding as it comes. Your emotions can get the best of you, lead you to decisions you didn't fully want to make. It can affect the consistency of relationships and sometimes places of work.

In this state, there are times you look back on a decision and think, "What was I thinking?" or "Why did I respond that way?" Well, you were living in your emotions, living in the moment of your desires and gut responses.

My emotions are a sign of my humanity, but my response to them is a sign of my maturity. When I mismanage my feelings, they in return manage me. And when they manage me, I mismanage my life. My emotions are meant to be indicators, not leaders. Emotions are like the lights on the dashboard of a car, indicating something is going on and you need to dive deeper and check under the hood.

Both of these responses are not helpful to our human experience and for sure not helpful to our walk with Jesus. Both ends of those emotional responses are not going to lead us to emotional health. Shoving our emotions does not help us nor does fully living in them and obeying them.

There is a better way, a middle ground, that the way of Jesus offers. A way to fully be in tune with your emotions, your desires and your thoughts, but to not bow down to them and give them full control.

There is a way to surrender them to Jesus, live in an emotionally healthy way, and have balance in your inner world.

YOU ARE TRIUNE BEING

I don't know where you stand currently on your religious background or lack thereof. If you have made it this far after all this Jesus and scripture talk, I am thankful you didn't quit yet and burn the book. If you made it thus far, maybe some questions about God are starting to stir in your heart.

I'm sure you have figured it out, but I believe all humans were made in the image of God. I believe humans weren't made because of evolution, the world wasn't made because atoms ran into each other and created a ball of gas. I believe the world was made on purpose with a purpose, and so were humans.

Humans were made in the image of God. We are the imago dei. This is a Latin phrase that means 'the image of God,' and it describes the verse from Genesis 1:26. In that verse there is a Hebrew word image that is the equivalent of our English word 'idol.' What is an idol? It is a physical representation of the invisible God it serves.

We are God's idols, his images. When people see us they should see Yahweh.

This God that we are called to resemble has three persons to him: God the father, God the son, and God the Holy Spirit. Yahweh is a triune being.

So therefore, we were made as triune beings. We have a body, a soul, and a spirit.

Your body makes you world conscious. To hug, touch, feel, to be in contact with others. Our body connects us to the world around us.

Your soul makes you self conscious. Your soul is your mind, will and emotions. Your soul makes you aware of you, it makes you aware of your inner being and world. As we have been talking about, being aware of the state of your soul is of utmost importance

Your spirit makes you God conscious. Your spirit is the side of you that gets saved immediately when you start following Jesus. It is the regenerated and redeemed part of your being. Your soul and body are in a process of being saved, and will be completely saved on the day of Jesus' return But your spirit is saved immediately and fully when you start following Jesus. It is the most God-like part of your being.

Every day you get to choose what part of you leads. All three of those areas of your being are fighting for leadership. When you let your soul and body lead, we usually end up in places we don't want to be. But when we let our spirit lead, the most God-like part of us, we end up where God wants us to be.

Here is a funny question, but nonetheless very real: Do you think you are better at humanity than Jesus?

Yes, I know it seems a bit pharisaical to even ask it, but I want you to think about it. Because I think some of us subconsciously believe this.

Some of us believe that now that you are a Christian, you are going to just float through life. Float through pain. On some level, you think that you are now untouchable because you are so spiritual. As if your humanity has now ceased and you are purely spiritual?

This view is not consistent with the narrative of scripture nor the narrative of the life of Jesus.
If Jesus, the best human to ever live and to offer the perfect example for the spiritual and Christian walk, had deep emotions like this, why do you think you aren't allowed to?
Do you think that showing deep seated emotions like anger, depression and anxiety is a lack of spirituality? If that's true, what do you think of Jesus? You must not think highly of him in this Gethsemane story then.

But that's not the case, it can't be.

Jesus is showing us how to be human. Real humans. When you are following Jesus fully with your emotions, surrendering them to Him, and letting your spirit lead your body and soul, you will begin to encounter God in new and deeper ways.

JESUS SHOWS US HOW TO PRAY

I have three children that are currently 11, 9, and 3. The two older ones are now full blown humans. Now it's no longer about just keeping them alive, now it's about actually raising them. At this age they have personalities, skills and abilities, wills, ideals for life, etc. They think they are functioning adults. Now that they are older, all they want to do is talk. When they start a story, I hope you have three hours of your life blocked out, because it takes a 9-year old girl that long to finish a story, along with the 23 stories within that story.

I love it and it's a thorn in my side, simultaneously.

If my daughter came up to me and started talking in Old English, calling me King Andrew, telling me all kinds of nonsense and facts, while i knew for a fact that she had just got bullied at school and that's what was really on her heart, I would be thinking, "Why are you telling me these random facts? This is not what's on your heart. I know what you really want to talk about, so just talk to me like your father."

Do you notice Jesus' dialogue in prayer with God the Father? Three different times Jesus asked for this cup to pass.

Not once. Not twice. But three times, Jesus tells God the father, "I don't want to do this."

Jesus does not shy away from his real emotions and real desires. This is not Jesus being fake humble either, just saying what he thinks he is supposed to say to look humble, like he really does want to drink this cup, but is acting like he doesn't.

That is not what is happening. Think about how profound this is. Jesus is saying no. He is telling God about something he does not want to do.

In this moment, you are seeing the full divinity and humanity of Jesus on display. Jesus knows exactly what is about to happen in the coming hours. He is fully God and fully man. He knows the suffering that is coming, but he is also scared of it, and does not want it. He does not want to suffer the brutal death that is lurking in his future.

And he tells God the father how he actually feels.

What do you think prayer is? Do you think prayer is the place you go to tell God what you think he wants to hear?

Is prayer the place you go to fake it, be pious and humble, mumbling words toward the heavens to please God?

Or is prayer the place you go to be honest, having your soul bare before the Lord, and saying what your heart is really feeling?

I think for some us prayer is the place we go to escape from real life. It's where we go to this other fantasy world and pray about things that don't matter, things that our heart is not filled with, just to avoid what is really going on down here in real time. Then we end our solemn moments of just "praying" and come back to earth.

It's almost like prayer is the place we go to lie to ourselves and to God.

That's not what prayer was meant to be. Not the way Jesus prayed at least, nor the way he showed us to pray.

You see, prayer is not the place we go to avoid reality, prayer is the place we go to face reality.

Prayer should be the place where we go in full honesty and talk to God about what's deep in our heart.

This is why Jesus says in Matt 6:5-8 *"When you pray, don't be like the hypocrites who love to pray publicly on street corners and in the synagogues where everyone can see them. I tell you the truth, that is all the reward they will ever get.* ***6*** *But when you pray, go away by yourself, shut the door behind you, and pray to your Father in private. Then your Father, who sees everything, will reward you.* ***7*** *"When you pray, don't babble on and on as the Gentiles do. They think their prayers are answered merely by repeating their words again and again.* ***8*** *Don't be like them, for your Father knows exactly what you need even before you ask him!"*

When you think prayer is simply uttering religious words, no wonder many Christian's don't pray. No wonder prayer is viewed as boring, rigid, and in most cases useless.

One of the greatest christian authors was EM Bounds, in his book on prayer he says,"Prayer is not a duty which must be performed, but rather as a privilege to be enjoyed, a rare delight that is always revealing some new beauty."

When you are early in your prayer life, it might start as a discipline, but it will turn into delight. It might start as something you need to cultivate and grow a hunger in, but the more you grow and the more you get to know God, prayer will turn into a delight and a joy, not a task.

Words don't move God's heart. Your heart moves God's heart. He wants you, not your pious and holy words. He wants the fullness of your heart, mind and soul present when you talk to him. Like a good father.

Jesus is showing us how to pray. How to really pray. Even in the face of pain and suffering.
Jesus is showing us how to pray completely and honestly. He tells God the father three times he does not want this cup, but also ends every prayer with, "but your will be done, not mine."

He is fully honest about his emotions and his desires, but he also submits his will. Prayer is both, not one or the other.

It is being fully open to God, being honest, telling him what is really going on in your heart and what you really want, and it is simultaneously saying you want his will over yours.
God does not want you to flush your will down the toilet and act like you don't have one: he wants you to keep your will and learn how to submit it.

Let's go back to that text in Matthew 6 and look at how Jesus finishes this sermon on prayer. This text is the most famous text on prayer in the New Testament and has been named the Lord's Prayer for centuries. Christians around the world pray this every day.

"Our Father in heaven, hallowed be your name. 10 Your kingdom come, your will be done, on earth as it is in heaven.11 Give us this day our daily bread, 12 and forgive us our debts, as we also have forgiven our debtors.13 And lead us not into temptation, but deliver us from evil."

I don't know about you, but to me that transition in the prayer seems like such a large jump. We go from the majesty and holiness of God's name and his kingdom, to daily bread? From the kingdom of God to lunch?

Why? Because our life is made up of both of them. The greatness and holiness of God and his kingdom, and the smallness of the need of daily food, go hand in hand.

In the garden of gethsemane Jesus is showing us this prayer in one short sentence. Prayer is both making God's name holy, praying his will not yours, his kingdom not yours, and also praying for your daily bread, your forgiveness, and your temptation.

I believe daily bread has to do with more than just literal food. Though it absolutely is that, it's also more than that. I believe daily bread is the things we need in our life, the things we are lacking. That part of the prayer is us being honest with our needs and desires.

LESSONS FROM JOB

One of the craziest books in the Bible is the book of Job. To me, it's a theological mine field. It presents so many problems to the human heart and mind. Chapter 1 alone is so hard to wrap my mind around theologically, the scene that is being portrayed with God, the devil and Job.

There are many lessons in the book of job and many, many argument points of the human experience and the picture of the goodness of God.

One of the major themes in the book of Job is how we talk to God.

Here's a 30,000 foot overview of the book:

There are 42 chapters in the book of job. Chapter 1 is setting the scene and premise of the story. Then chapters 2 through 39 are about Job and his three friends talking. That's right, the majority of the book about pain and suffering in the Bible is about how you and your friends talk during seasons of pain, and the entire time, God is listening.

Job's three friends are not great friends; they are actually kind of the worst. They are not the friends you want around you during death and loss, but they say good things about God, for the most part. Most of their claims about God are true.

Job, on the other hand, says horrible things about God and to God. Things I didn't know you were ever allowed to vocalize to God. Things that I thought if you did, God's thunder bolt was on the way. He says things that are untrue about God, theologically wrong about God, and incredibly disrespectful and arrogant.

At the end of the book God finally speaks up. And it's not what you think it's going to be.
You would assume that he is about to blast Job to smithereens and thank his friends for the kind words.

But that is not what happens at all. The exact opposite actually. God royally destroys his three friends and their words to Him, and honors Job.

Job 42:8 says, "My servant Job will pray for you, and I will accept his prayer and not deal with you according to your folly. You have not spoken the truth about Me, as my servant Job has."

Wait, wait, wait.

How is that possibly true? God, did you listen to the whole conversation? You heard what Job said about you and to you, how could you say that job has honored you and spoken the truth?
If you listen to their conversation from chapters 2-39, you will probably not notice a very subtle but profound truth: the three friends never talk to God, they only talk about God. Job talks directly to God. See, all the evil and horrible things Job said, they were said to God, not to others about God.

Because prayer is where you go to talk to God, not about Him. God doesn't mind what you have to say, just say it TO him.

God doesn't mind your anger, your questions, even your deep resentment about His own character, just say it to Him.

God wants to hear your heart. Your real heart. He wants to have a real and genuine conversation with you. He doesn't want some fake and polished relationship with his children, no father does.

He wants you. All of you. The good and the bad, the ugly and the beautiful. Even more so during seasons of trials and suffering. Don't run away from Him, run toward him.

Do you see what comes out in the prayer of Jesus in the garden? *"Yet not my will be done but your will."*

During seasons like the garden of gethsemane, what is made very clear in your prayers is whether you have a covenant with God or a contract with God.

Jesus does not say, "If you don't take this away from me and remove this suffering, I will not follow you." No Jesus says even if his way, his will, his desires, are not fulfilled, he is still surrendered and he will still follow God.

Unfortunately for many followers of Jesus, this is not the case with our relationship with him. We have more of a contract with God than a covenant. If you do these things, God, I'm in and I will continue to follow, but if these things don't happen I'm out.

That is not a healthy recipe for any friendship, marriage, or spirituality.

Pain and suffering have a special way of revealing how we truly feel about God. Losing something you greatly care about has a way of ripping off anything fake or forced; it is incredibly revealing.

When life doesn't go your way, and you feel like God is not holding up his part, what does that do to your faith? What does that do to your view of God and his goodness?

I don't want a contract with God, I want a deep covenant with him. That no matter how low the lows are, I'm here, I'm not going anywhere.

JESUS IS SHOWING US HOW TO LIVE IN TWO PLACES AT ONCE

Being raised in church my whole life, having both sides of my family being pastors, only God knows how many church gatherings I have been in. Retreats, advances, conferences, all night prayer nights, Saturday prayer, Sunday after church pot luck, the list never ends. If I don't get into heaven just based on my church attendance I'm in big trouble.

Being in that many church services, I have heard thousands of sermons in my life. I was the pastor's kid that would fall asleep in the front row, wake up two hours later, and the same sermon is still going.

Because of that reality, I have heard these passages from the Garden of Gethsemene preached on before, numerous times, from many different angles. But I have never before seen the things in the text that I am about to share with you, nor remember it being preached. Maybe it was said and I never paid attention? But even if I had heard it, the truths would never have stuck in my mind or heart.

However, as I have walked through the last few years and such a deep season of pain, this Gethsemene story became alive to me. All of these truths and principles were there all along, I just hadn't seen them or paid close enough attention. But now my eyes and heart were open to a whole new reality in this text. What we are about to talk about, in my opinion, is one of the most profound revelations in this story.

No hyperbole or preacher jargon. This revelation changed my life. It changed me. It deeply formed my perspective on pain and suffering.

Jesus is teaching how to live in the present while knowing the future. That is to say—he is showing us how to live in tension with two truths at the same time.

Not to insult your theological intelligence, but let's remind ourselves of two very foundational doctrines. First, we believe that Jesus is God. He wasn't just a good man, a prophet, or a moral revolutionist. He was God in the flesh.

He is also fully man. He ate, drank, got tired, got angry, had friends, brothers and sisters. He was fully human.

He wasn't just God with skin on, floating through the human existence like some demigod, void of all human emotions and realities.

He is fully God and fully human. Not 50% God and 50% human, lower half God and upper half human. No, he was fully both. In one body. Simultaneously.

Yes, I know that is a massive claim and hard to wrap our little finite brains around. But that's one of the core orthodox doctrines.

Maybe you don't agree with that doctrine or have many questions, as do I, but we don't have time to unpack that argument today.

For the sake of time, go with me around the idea that we all agree to that claim and believe it.

Let's use deductive reasoning and just walk through this for a moment…

Okay so that means, while Jesus is in this garden of pain, while he is downcast, distraught, sweating blood, and his soul is anguished, he is fully God and fully man. So while he is having this unbelievably human experience of pain and suffering, he is also fully God during this moment in time.

Jesus doesn't switch back and forth between God and man. It's not like while he is healing people he is fully God but in this moment he is fully man, while the God side of him is shut off.

In this moment of pain, he is fully God.

So, wait a second. That means if he is fully God, he knows all, he is omniscient. He knows the future. He knows how this is going to end. He knows in a few days he will resurrect on Easter Sunday, so who cares about Good Friday?

So that is to say—he is living in Friday, but he also knows Sunday is coming.

He knows he will resurrect, he knows he is going to defeat hell, death and the grave. He knows this ends in victory and dominion, not defeat.

So why isn't Jesus happy?! Why isn't he celebrating in this garden?!

If this was happening in real time in an American church the sermon would go something like this:

"Take courage Jesus! Yes, the pain is real, and suffering is present, but who cares?!

Resurrection is a few days away! Fix your focus, Jesus! Don't focus on today, focus on what is coming!"

While that sermon has some truth in it, it is not helpful. At all. Jesus does not teach us that in this story, nor does he preach that sermon.

Though Jesus knew it was going to be okay, he was allowing himself not to be okay. Yes, he knew Sunday was coming, but Friday is still real. He knew resurrection was coming, but that didn't erase the fact that death was around the corner.

You see, as Christ followers, yes, we know how the book ends, yes, we know every tear will be wiped and every cancer healed. Yes, we know Jesus has won and will win again at the end of time, and he is victorious and all will be made well. Amen. That is true and good.

But that truth does not negate the reality of the pain today, the suffering right now is still painful. You see, the reality of Sunday does not erase the reality of Friday.

This deeply changed me. Watching Jesus in this garden formed my understanding of pain and suffering so much.

It is not a lack of faith or a lack of trust in Jesus to admit you are in pain, you are angry, your soul is crushed and you feel like giving up. All the while knowing it's going to be okay, you are going to make it, and Jesus will see you through to the other end.

This is a tension we must learn how to hold.

This is not the first time Jesus has shown us this either. There is this famous story in John chapter 11 with some of Jesus' best friends, Mary, Martha and Lazarus. Jesus actually spends a great deal of time with this family. In this story, Jesus again is teaching us how to respond to pain and suffering.

John 11:22-35 reads, "Martha said to Jesus, "Lord, if only you had been here, my brother would not have died. **22** But even now I know that God will give you whatever you ask."

23 Jesus told her, "Your brother will rise again."

24 "Yes," Martha said, "he will rise when everyone else rises, at the last day."

25 Jesus told her, "I am the resurrection and the life. Anyone who believes in me will live, even after dying. **26** Everyone who lives in me and believes in me will never ever die. Do you believe this, Martha?"

27 "Yes, Lord," she told him. "I have always believed you are the Messiah, the Son of God, the one who has come into the world from God." **28** Then she returned to Mary. She called Mary aside from the mourners and told her, "The Teacher is here and wants to see you." **29** So Mary immediately went to him.

30 Jesus had stayed outside the village, at the place where Martha met him. **31** When the people who were at the house consoling Mary saw her leave so hastily, they assumed she was going to Lazarus's grave to weep. So they followed her there. **32** When Mary arrived and saw Jesus, she fell at his feet and said, "Lord, if only you had been here, my brother would not have died."

33 When Jesus saw her weeping and saw the other people wailing with her, a deep anger welled up within him,[f] and he was deeply troubled. **34** "Where have you put him?" he asked them.

They told him, "Lord, come and see." **35** Then Jesus wept.

Again I ask the question: if Jesus is fully God, and knows the future, why is he weeping? He knows in about 30 seconds from this moment he is going to resurrect Lazarus from the dead. He knows that Martha and Mary's pain is about to end, the sorrow is about to cease, and their brother will live again.

Jesus does not show up on the scene, knowing what he is about to do, and tell them to stop the crying and stop the mourning.

He weeps with them. He feels deeply in this moment. At the same time knowing he is about to fix everything.

Absolutely powerful.

Jesus is showing us how to be human, and furthermore he is showing us how to be a true disciple.

A disciple of Jesus does not reject today's pain and sorrow knowing tomorrow is coming. We are invited to sit in our pain, in our trials of suffering, being fully present. All the while holding onto the hope of tomorrow.

The truth is today is painful. Horrible. The loss is unbearable. The anger is so real.

The truth is tomorrow is coming. Heaven is real. Victory is yours. Every wrong will be made right. God has the final say, the cancer does not.

Jesus is inviting you to come and wrestle with these two truths. Come and fight with the tension. Because Jesus did.

Let's change positions for a little bit. We have been talking about ourselves for a few chapters now.

How do you handle other people's pain? This is as important a question to answer as it is to answer the question of how to handle your own pain.

How do you typically respond to other people's pain and suffering? Are you quick to hold them, sit with them, cry with them? Are you quick to tell them to suck it up, that others have it worse and life will get better soon. Are you quick to listen or quick to fix it and tell them answers?

Are you the type of Christian that I have been talking about, that unknowingly or knowingly dismisses people's pain because "heaven is real, God is on the throne," and essentially telling people to get over it?

Let me say it another way: are you a safe person with other people's pain?

Christine Pohl wrote an amazing book on the practice of hospitality. The book is called "Making Room" and it is about how followers of Jesus should practice hospitality in their homes, around tables, and how we do life together in community.

There is one section of the book that she writes about how some Christians are very hospitable with their homes and meals, but they aren't hospitable with the people in their homes, especially around peoples pain.

She says one of the major aspects of being a good host is allowing room for people's pain and suffering to be at the dinner table. A place for people to open the flood gates of their heart, and have it be welcomed and cared for.

She writes, *"Although as a society we seem enamored with those who project self-confidence and offer ready answers to even the most complex questions, the best hosts are people who recognize their own frailties and weaknesses. If we need to hide either, we are unlikely to offer much hospitality. Hospitality to strangers, especially when practiced in community, has a way of laying bare our lives and surfacing our inadequacies"*

To be hospitable to people, it is not just physically, it is emotionally as well.

To be honest, before my whole world fell apart when I was 26, I was that person. I was quick to dismiss people and their pain. I would give them Bible verses to go memorize, prayers to write on their mirrors, and essentially told them to get over it in nice pastoral language.

I didn't understand how they could be this depressed, anxious, and angry knowing Jesus won and heaven will fix everything. Unfortunately, back then my disposition was that life is hard, so suck it up, and keep it moving.

Until it happened to me. Until life ruined my veneer view of pain. Life humbled me. I hadn't really experienced much pain in life until 26. Life was relatively easy before that year. People who haven't suffered much are likely to have naïve stories about life's meaning. People who have never experienced need or marginality, or who are uncomfortable with their own vulnerability, often find it easy to ignore everyone else's.

One of the most beautiful results of pain and suffering, is it gives you a new grace and a new heart to walk with people through theirs. It not only changes how you relate to yourself, but to everyone around you.

NAVIGATING DISAPPOINTMENT

For the fourth truth that we can learn from Jesus' life, I want to talk about how to navigate disappointment. As I've mentioned, when I was walking with my dad through a grueling cancer diagnosis, I was dealing with so many other parts of my life. I've written how I was newly married with a brand new son, and how my boss had just tragically died. But what I haven't shared yet is that ALSO I was in full-time ministry and that my father-in-law had just been sentenced to prison. I know. Even as I write all that, it's a LOT.

To say life was overwhelming would be an understatement. I was trying to juggle all of that amidst my dad going through chemo treatments, not really knowing if he was going to make it or not. Looking back, I don't even think I knew what was fully going on. I went into autopilot, just surviving each day. Truthfully, I was just avoiding it all, not wanting to talk about it, or even really knowing how to talk about it. I emotionally and, in some ways, relationally shut down.

During that season I felt incredibly disappointed and frustrated. My wife and I didn't feel like we were getting cared for, our friends weren't there for us, we were just dropped, and left to fend for ourselves.

I thought a situation like that would go so differently. I just expected so much to happen in a season like that,

that just never came. I would wait and wait, and it just never happened.

I became very angry and I lost hope in relationships. I felt aimless and lost for the first time in my life. We were drowning with no rescue boats anywhere to be seen.

For me, one of the more difficult aspects of pain and suffering is navigating disappointment in your friends and family. Disappointed they didn't do more, say more, be there for you in a more real and tangible way.

It's one thing to feel let down by God, feeling like God wasn't as good as you thought he should be, and your faith beginning to waver. But God is invisible and it doesn't hit your heart the same as when your brother and sisters, or your best friend, your pastor, or a mentor you are really close to, let you down. It hits different. It hurts. It makes the suffering worse, makes it deeper, like the wind got kicked out of you.

When you get the phone call, open the letter, hear the diagnosis, it's a crushing moment. Your world begins to spin out of control. But if you live within a good community of people, your mind typically goes to "well, this is going to be incredibly difficult, but thank God i have *them* in my life." And when those faces you see in your mind don't step up and step in, when they aren't there how you thought they would be, it's soul crushing at the deepest level.

I think I felt a lot like how Jesus felt in the garden of Gethsemane. In this story we have been unpacking together, you see Jesus' disappointment in his friends, and you actually see it three times.

Look again at Matthew 26
40 *Then he returned to the disciples and found them asleep. He said to Peter, "Couldn't you watch with me even one hour?* ***41*** *Keep watch and pray, so that you will not give in to temptation. For the spirit is willing, but the body is weak!"*

42 *Then Jesus left them a second time and prayed, "My Father! If this cup cannot be taken away unless I drink it, your will be done."* ***43*** *When he returned to them again, he found them sleeping, for they couldn't keep their eyes open.*

Jesus is in the darkest moment of his life thus far, his soul is crushed within him, he does not want to go to the cross, he is sweating blood from fear and worry. He finally gets his three best friends alone for a moment, asks them to pray for him, and they fall asleep on him.

Imagine this scene and how emotionally and relationally discouraging it would be. Jesus is asking for support from his best friends, for some prayer in a horrible moment, and his friends fall asleep on him, three different times.

I think you can hear it in Jesus' voice when he says, "can you not even watch with me for one hour?" I truly don't think his tone was anger or yelling at him, i think his voice was soft and disappointed in his friends. I don't even think he was disappointed in his disciples, but in his friends.

You see, one of the things you are going to experience during seasons of pain and suffering is being let down by your friends and family. For sure some will be there, you will have support and some friends you weren't even close to will step up and be a surprise to you. Don't mishear me, I'm not saying all seasons of pain and suffering you will be utterly alone, so you better get used to it, because no one will be there for you. No, you will definitely have people surrounding you. It's just painful when it's not the ones you thought it would be.

I would like to personally submit I think it's good for you that this happens. I think it's actually a benefit to you, and a good thing that people disappoint you, and you don't have those around you that you thought you would.

Because it makes you lean into God in a deeper way, in a way you wouldn't have if you would've had the support.

I want to jump over to Luke's gospel and read this story in his words, because each gospel writer is telling the same story from a different angle. Luke gives us a detail that is deeply profound that Matthew does not.

Luke 22:39-45 says, "Then, accompanied by the disciples, Jesus left the upstairs room and went as usual to the Mount of Olives. **40** *There he told them, "Pray that you will not give in to temptation."* **41** *He walked away, about a stone's throw, and knelt down and prayed,* **42** *"Father, if you are willing, please take this cup of suffering away from me. Yet I want your will to be done, not mine."* **43** *Then an angel from heaven appeared and strengthened him.* **44** *He prayed more fervently, and he was in such agony of spirit that his sweat fell to the ground like great drops of blood.* **45** *At last he stood up again and returned to the disciples, only to find them asleep, exhausted from grief"*

Same story with majority of the same details, except one major one. Luke's account has the same situation, Jesus is praying in the garden, and the disciples are sleeping, and he is getting no help and no support from them. But who does come and give Jesus support?

An Angel from heaven comes and strengthens him.

Sometimes in certain seasons of pain and suffering, you don't need earthly help, you need heavenly help.

I don't think the disciples were bad friends, I don't think they were purposely leaving Jesus out to dry, I just think they couldn't help. They didn't know what to do.

Furthermore, I don't think Jesus needed their help; it wouldn't have sufficed. In this garden, in this moment, Jesus didn't need earthly help, he needed heavenly help.

Yes, there are going to be some moments in life when you feel disappointed, let down, dropped, and anger starts ruling your heart. But friends, I submit you are not being pushed out of peoples lives, you are being pulled into God's.

God is trying to use this dark dark moment in your life to draw you to himself. Because what you actually need in this season is God. What you actually need is his comfort, his words, his embrace.

The truth is there is some pain so deep, earthly help doesn't suffice, it just doesn't get the job done. It's like a bandaid on a bullet wound.

I can't explain to you what the revelation from these verses did to my heart.

It healed memories. It healed my heart. It healed my perspective of people. It healed, well, me.

As I've stated above, back then I felt like we were let down, we were dropped. But now, looking back, that's not totally true. I was being drawn in by God. He was calling me to himself, in a deeper way.

Looking back now some 10 years later, a little older and a little wiser, I am so thankful for that season. It changed my life. During that season I learned God's voice, I found a new relationship to the scriptures, and I learned more about God's character than from any other season previously. I learned more about myself and who I was becoming.

Have you felt like this? Do you feel like this right now? Are you looking around your life asking where everyone is? Why aren't people helping me like they should be? If disappointment has seeped into your heart and mind, and if you're not careful to address those feelings, it will turn into resentment.

I'm here to encourage someone reading this. There is no question you will learn how to navigate disappointment.

Unfortunately there is no doubt one of the difficult truths will be that it will change the status of some relationships. Maybe some relationships that you thought would be by your side forever, but life has changed that reality. This is a painful pill to swallow.

But I would like to lay at your feet, during the pain of others walking out on you, God is trying to draw you to himself. God is trying to use this opportunity to get closer to you. To show you that is truly closer than a brother.

Maybe, just maybe, God has you right where he wants you. Alone. No where to run, no one to talk to, no one to lean on.

But Him.

He is waiting for you to choose him.

HIDING IN COMMUNITY

Every one of us handle pain and suffering differently, in all areas: emotionally, mentally, physically, relationally. When tough seasons enter our life, we can avoid it, run and hide, scream, drink, shop, eat, flat out ignore it, deny it. We all choose different escapes.

When I want to hide, I get busy. Busy with friends, my kids, my job, anything will do, just whatever keeps me distracted. The busier I am the less I have to think, the less I have to answer questions my soul is asking. The busier I am, the more I can say "everything is fine" and kind of believe it.

I don't know about you, but for me, physically busy means emotionally absent.

So maybe you're like me, you try to hide in community. Get lost in people, parties, road trips, backyard bbq. If you do this, you can start to think, this is good. I am surrounded by friends and family during this painful season, I am leaning into my community.

But the reality is, you have hijacked your community, using it to avoid yourself. Your community has become your hostage. You can lean into community and it can look like a strength, but it is only a cover up from the one trying to hide from himself and his inner world.

From his book "Life Together" *Dietrich Bonhoeffer says,"many seek fellowship because they are afraid to be alone."*

Community during pain and suffering is a massive aspect of surviving, don't mishear me. But what I'm saying is we can't use them to avoid doing the deep work of internal investigations and conversations.

There is a big difference between solitude and isolation. Isolation is when you are running from something; solitude is when you are running toward someone.

I am not encouraging you to run away from your community, go into isolation and hide and spend your time talking to yourself.

No, that can do great damage and many times make pain and suffering much worse.

I am encouraging you to get away with yourself and God. To lean into your heavenly help, your Heavenly Father.

I pray you allow this story of Jesus to help you let go of some people you have been expecting so much from, and lean into God. Lean into his presence and his Word. If you need the voice and encouragement of people more than God, you will run yourself ragged trying to find it. You will spend years of your life chasing something you will not find, looking for something only God can give you.

Henry Nouwan in his book A Spirituality for Living, he writes, "Why is it so important that solitude comes before community? If we do not know we are the beloved sons and daughters of God, we're going to expect someone in the community to make us feel that way, and they cannot. You have to listen to the voice who calls you the beloved, because otherwise you will run around begging for affirmation, for praise, for success. And then you're not free"

Nouwan is absolutely correct. We need to know who we are in God before we know who we are in community. Times of pain and suffering is where that happens. It's where we draw close to God. Learn about him and ourselves in deeper ways.

When you look at the life of Jesus in the four gospels, he spent a great deal of time with these 12 Jewish boys, and he also always had crowds chasing him. He was around people constantly.

But the Bible also gives frequent details about how often Jesus withdrew to be alone, either in the desert or the mountain tops. He would withdraw from the business of life to be with God. Jesus did not hide in his demeaning schedule. He didn't let people distract him from his inner life.

Jesus knew who he was, and even though his friends let him down when he needed them the most, they didn't shatter his identity. He didn't lose his way because they let him down. He didn't deconstruct because the church failed him. He leaned into His Father even more.

Jesus had to navigate disappointment and so will you. Jesus was let down by his closest friends and so will you.

Take courage though, friends, God is closer than you think. His presence is near. He is in the garden with you, waiting for you to lean in.

What I have been trying to communicate is that pain affects every single part of your life. You don't get to compartmentalize pain and suffering. We don't get to make back alley deals with pain, "Okay, pain, here are the three areas you're allowed to affect, but you are not allowed access in this part of my life." We know pain has no boundaries, we know it doesn't work that way, but sometimes we act as though it does. Pain affects all of you. It affects your relationships, your emotions, your thoughts and inner world, the way you view God, the way you talk to God, it touches everything.

WHY DOES GOD ALLOW PAIN AND SUFFERING?

YOUR PAIN IS WORKING FOR YOU

The majority of this book has been talking about what pain is, how it affects us, and how we get through dark seasons of suffering. As we get ready to wrap up this book, I want to shift focus and talk about what pain and suffering actually produces in you.

If I'm going through tough seasons like that, I'm not coming out empty handed. I want something from it. If pain and suffering are unavoidable, then I want it to produce something within me.

When you think of people in the biblical narrative that suffered a great deal, outside of Jesus of Nazareth, the Apostle Paul is arguably the one who went through the most. In one of his letters, Paul lists out all of the suffering he has endured while following Jesus: imprisoned multiple times, whipped five different times, beaten with rods three different times, stoned with rocks, shipwrecked three different times, beaten and robbed. Now that is a list! Talk about pain and suffering! Some of the western church thinks persecution is when someone is mean to you on social media for being a Christian and unfollows you. Let's be honest, if half of that list happened to us, we would quit. We would deconstruct our faith, we would blame God, and we would walk out of the church and never come back. We would want to quit on life as a whole. Not the Apostle Paul.

Paul had every reason to say God isn't good, following Jesus isn't worth it, how could this happen to me, but he didn't. Paul never allowed the "woe is me" narrative to come on his life. He was a man of deep pain and suffering, yet was also the man who wrote two-thirds of the New Testament, planted churches all over the then known world, and changed church history as we know it.

He writes in his second letter to the Corinthians about this suffering, and what it is producing. Sometimes I believe the pain is so deep, the loss is so great, our vision is so blurred, we have forgotten that our pain is actually producing something in us. Our pain did not just take from us; it is also giving us something in return.

I want to take a look for a moment about what your pain is producing in you, through the eyes of Paul.

2 Cor 4:7-18 says, "But we have this treasure in jars of clay to show that this all-surpassing power is from God and not from us. ***8*** *We are hard pressed on every side, but not crushed; perplexed, but not in despair;* ***9*** *persecuted, but not abandoned; struck down, but not destroyed.* ***10*** *We always carry around in our body the death of Jesus, so that the life of Jesus may also*

be revealed in our body. ***11*** *For we who are alive are*
always being given over to death for Jesus' sake, so
that his life may also be revealed in our mortal body. ***12***
So then, death is at work in us, but life is at work in you.
13 *It is written: "I believed; therefore I have spoken."*
Since we have that same spirit of faith, we also believe
and therefore speak, ***14*** *because we know that the one*
who raised the Lord Jesus from the dead will also raise
us with Jesus and present us with you to himself. ***15*** *All*
this is for your benefit, so that the grace that is reach-
ing more and more people may cause thanksgiving to
overflow to the glory of God. ***16*** *Therefore we do not*
lose heart. Though outwardly we are wasting away, yet
inwardly we are being renewed day by day. ***17*** *For our*
light and momentary troubles are achieving for us an
eternal glory that far outweighs them all. ***18*** *So we fix*
our eyes not on what is seen, but on what is unseen,
since what is seen is temporary, but what is unseen
is eternal"

I believe and so does the Apostle Paul, pain will produce amazing things in your life, if you will let it.

Here's a few things it will do:

PAIN PRODUCES NEW PERSEVERANCE

A few years ago Arizona University did a fascinating study on the growth of trees. They did a study growing trees in nature, and then created a multi-billion dollar Biodome called "The Biosphere 2". The project was created as a research tool for scientists to study Earth's living systems, and it allowed scientists to play with farming and innovation in a way that didn't harm the planet. **Here is a fascinating short excerpt from the article "The Necessity of Stress":**

"One of the most profound discoveries made by the scientists is a shocking one. The discovery had to do with the wind's role in a tree's life. The trees inside Biosphere 2 grew rapidly, more rapidly than they did outside of the dome, but they also fell over before reaching maturation. They grew incredibly faster than normal trees outside in nature, but they also fell over quickly. After looking at the root systems and outer layers of bark, the scientists came to realize that a lack of wind in Biosphere 2 caused a deficiency of stress wood. Stress wood helps a tree position itself for optimal sun absorption and it also helps trees grow more solidly. Without stress wood, a tree can grow quickly, but it cannot support itself fully. It cannot withstand normal wear and tear, and survive. In other words, the trees needed some stress in order to thrive in the long run. The study revealed a powerful

truth—it's the wind in the tree's life that makes it strong enough to not only grow tall, but to survive the seasons of life. The wind stresses the wood and makes it stronger each season, creating the tree with the durability to live for a long time, even during severe storms."

Profound discovery.

Could the same principle be true in human lives? I deeply believe so. It's the winds of life, the hardships and the stress of life, that actually makes us stronger and more durable. Without wind in our lives, we won't be able to endure the pain and difficulty of life. To avoid the wind is to actually damage the tree. To avoid pain and suffering is actually wreaking havoc on your life.

Yes the storms of life are painful, difficult, and when the winds blow in our life, it's hard not to fall down and quit. But it's those very same situations that, if we allow them to, can make us strong and durable in this life.

Whatever pain you are experiencing right now, or whatever the pain from the past, I pray it is producing a grit in you. Not bitterness, not a hard heart or an angry spirit, but a real perseverance in this life. I pray it creates a backbone in you that will not bend, and will not give up.

If you have been waving the white flag, put it down, and get back up and fight. We need you. We need what is in you. The world wont be the same without it. I know you're tired, I know it's been a long season, but there is a second or third wind coming to your lungs.

Let the pain, loss, devastation, and anger burn like a fire in your heart to motivate you to keep moving forward.

The cloud of witnesses is cheering you on. I am cheering you on.

If you will let it, pain will produce an unbelievable perseverance in you.

You can hear it in Paul's voice: "We are hard pressed on every side, but not crushed; perplexed, but not in despair; **9** persecuted, but not abandoned; struck down, but not destroyed"

This is a man who had a fight in him like few others. This man was not going to quit, he was not going to lay down. He had true perseverance, I hope it's being created within you as well. I

PAIN PRODUCES NEW CHARACTER

When the famous Michaelangelo finished the renowned image of David, someone asked him how he chiseled that image out of a block of marble. Michaelangelo replied famously, "Easy, you chip away every piece of stone that doesn't look like David".

The pain of the chisel upon our lives is not comfortable or pleasant, no one prays for it, but what comes from it, we pray for. It chisels away parts of our character, our perspective, and our way of life that needs to be removed.

Pain is the great chisel, that slowly but surely chips away the pieces that don't look like us, the real us. We must not forget that God lives outside of time; he is the alpha and the omega. So God sees you and your life from an eternal angle, not a temporal one. God already knows and sees what you can become, and it's from there that God speaks to you. The real you, not the current one, or the past one. He is calling you upward not backward, he is calling you into who you really are. Who he made you to be, not the you who this world wants to form you into.

God does not speak evil into this world, that would be against his character. And God cannot change, for that's what makes him God; he is immutable, that is to say, he is unchangeable.

But God will use pain and suffering as his tool, as his chisel. He will use situations and turn them around for his glory and his plan in our lives and his eternal mission.

As Joseph famously said in Genesis 50:20 after his brothers sold him into slavery, “what you meant for evil, God used for good”

What the devil meant for evil, what people around you meant for evil, God will turn it around and use it for good. God did not author it, but he will use it.

Look again at what Paul says in 2 Corinthians, “**16** So we do not lose heart. Though our outer self is wasting away, our inner self is being renewed day by day”.

So what is pain producing? You. Your character, your inner self, your spirit. It is being renewed every day. It is being strengthened and made strong.

You must catch this: the greatest gift you get from pain is the person you become. Who you become despite the loss, the people walking out on you, the suffering you did not deserve. Who you become in the middle of all that is the greatest reward.

Many people are driven by revenge after seasons of suffering, especially the pain done at the hand of others.

They want to get back, they want to get even, they want revenge.

We both know that doesn't work, and getting even doesn't fix much, except feeling validated for about five minutes. But what would a holy revenge look like? I would submit, it looks like becoming who God created you to be. Using the pain as fuel to the fire.

Pain and suffering are going to change you, you have no option. You will not be the same person after the dust settles and the tears stop flowing.

You will change. You have changed. And you know it.

But changed into what? Changed into who?

Well, that's your choice. That is in your power to make that decision. No one else can make it for you.

The seasons of pain I have written about in this book deeply changed me, for the better. I would never pray for those seasons, but I would also never exchange them. They are priceless to me. Those created a new person within me.

PAIN PRODUCES NEW HEART

My wife is an Italian from upstate New York and she was raised on old films, musicals and plays. She can sing you any old hymn and quote any black and white movie from the 30s. She has always been into musicals, while I, on the other hand, was not. Going to musicals was like nails on a chalk board. But I have grown to understand and appreciate them.

One of our trips to NYC we went to see Wicked on Broadway, and I have to admit, it was amazing. I was shocked by many things during the play, but one of them was where we were sitting. We were off to the right of the stage, up a few levels and so we could see some of the backstage crew and the madness that goes on behind the curtain.

It gave me a whole new perspective of these musicals. It is impressive what goes on behind the curtain: the changing of wardrobes, the scenes changing, the switching of props. But we wouldn't have seen all of that if we had sat in the middle of the audience..

Every seat has a perspective.

When you change seats, it gives you a whole different angle and view you did not have before.

Such is life. You can judge someone's opinion, perspective, or answers to life, but until you go sit in their seat, you don't understand.

Pain and suffering do the same thing. It changes us, deeply. Especially how we view others and their pain. I have learned pain will produce a new heart in you. Specifically, what I mean is a soft heart.

When you have been through the deep waters of life and experienced life-altering pain, it will either make you bitter or compassionate.

There is really no in between.

See, we just talked about perseverance, but don't mistake that for being hard and cruel. Acting like it's not there by yelling at people to suck it up, get over it, and fight through the pain.

That is not what I am speaking to. Don't let perseverance turn into harshness.

Pain has a very real way of humbling you, and when you see others suffering, your heart toward them changes. Not only does your heart toward them change, but also your answers toward them change. Pain gives you a new language. It is like learning a whole new dialect.

When you start talking to someone about pain and suffering, you can hear it in their words and their heart. Unfortunately, the same can be true of people who have never been through the deep waters of life, you hear it in their descriptions of life, you can sense the lack of awareness through their stories, there is a disconnection that is palpable.

Your heart is going to change, and you get to choose how. Do you want it to become hard and calloused, or soft and gentle?

I pray for a new level of compassion to come to your life, a new sense of empathy that you have never possessed before.

PAIN PRODUCES NEW VISION

When you read the New Testament, especially Paul and Peter's letters, you will find one topic that is repeated often: heaven. Paul and Peter are constantly reminding their fellow Christians to think about the kingdom of heaven, not the kingdom of earth.

We are seated there—Eph 2:6 "For he raised us from the dead along with Christ and seated us with him in the heavenly realms because we are united with Christ Jesus"

Our focus is there—Col 3:1-2 “Since you have been raised to new life with Christ, set your sights on the realities of heaven, where Christ sits in the place of honor at God’s right hand. Think about the things of heaven, not the things of earth”

Our king is there—1 Peter 3:22 “He has been raised to heaven and is seated at the right hand”

Our future is there—Heb 11 “We are foreigners on our way home to our heavenly homeland”

Our treasure is there—Matt 6:19 “Don’t store up treasures here on earth, where moths eat them and rust destroys them, and where thieves break in and steal. Store your treasures in heaven, where moths and rust cannot destroy, and thieves do not break in and steal. Wherever your treasure is, there the desires of your heart will also be”

Our citizenship is there—Phil 3:20 “But we are citizens of heaven, where the Lord Jesus Christ lives. And we are eagerly waiting for him to return as our Savior”

Just to name a few and there are many more. Heaven was a central theme for the early believers, and it must be for us.

Every one of us has different levels and experiences in our pain and suffering. If we both lost a loved one, how and why it happened, are completely different. So though the pain is similar it's not fully the same. Our pain and suffering, though it makes us feel seen and heard, it is not what unites us. Our past does not unite us, our future does. Heaven is our common hope.

Heaven should be the horizon every believer has their eye on and heart set toward. But sadly that is not the case for much of American Christianity. We have lost our North Star. We have forgotten this world is not our home, and that we are sojourners passing through to our eternal home. We have worked so hard trying to make this world our home, but it will never be so.

One of CS Lewis' most famous quotes and one of the core principles on why he became a believer was around the idea that this earth was not fulfilling his deepest longing. "If I find in myself desires which nothing in this world can satisfy, the only logical explanation is that I was made for another world."

Here is a good question you should ask yourself: How much of the hope of heaven informs your daily life as a Christian?

AW Tozer writes about this idea in his book "the incredible christian, "The spiritual man habitually makes eternity decisions instead of time decisions. If you read history you will find that the Christians who did most for the present world were precisely those who thought most of the next. It is since Christians have largely ceased to think of the other world that they have become so ineffective in this. The more heavenly minded you are, the more earthly good you are"

What drives your decisions? What informs your choices? Is it heaven or is it tomorrow?

That longing for a better tomorrow, is not random by the way. The reason every human being breathing on this planet has thought about eternity, what happens after you die, what the after life consists of, all of that is put there by your Creator, not your anxiety.

Ecc 3:11 teaches us, "Yet God has made everything beautiful for its own time. He has planted eternity in the human heart, but even so, people cannot see the whole scope of God's work from beginning to end"

God put those questions in your heart. God put that longing for something deeper in you. God knows the human condition, he knows we need a horizon, he knows we need something to fix our focus on, something to pull us through today. Friends I beg you, regularly draw your attention to heaven. Pray about heaven. Talk about heaven. Sing about heaven. Counsel each other from heaven's perspective. When you read the New Testament and the stories of our ancestors, heaven was not a side note or some random concept. It was the very thing that captured their thoughts, and informed everything that did on this earth.

Make heaven so much a part of your community and relationships, whether on the brightest day or the darkest night, so you can say with confidence, "Jesus is coming, and he will make this right. Once and for all. We are going home, where we belong."

Pain is producing in you a new vision, a new perspective, a new horizon to focus on. It lifts our eyes from the dust of the ground to the heavens above. It gets our focus off the earthly temporal things that lie before us and fixes our gaze on the eternal.

I would invite you into taking a moment, even putting this book down, and think about all of the things pain has produced in you. These were just a few simple ideas, I'm sure you could list out more in your own life.

You should slow down and take some inventory of your life. I would bet some of the things in you that you are most proud of, came from a difficult situation that produced something within you.

You can easily list out all of the things you lost, but what have you gained?

Do you see Paul's language in the text —"For this light momentary affliction is preparing for us an eternal weight of glory beyond all comparison, **18** as we look not to the things that are seen but to the things that are unseen. For the things that are seen are transient, but the things that are unseen are eternal"

This world is light but heaven is weighty
This world is momentary but heaven is eternal
This world is fully affliction heaven is full of glory

Receive a new vision today, receive a new focus. Set your eyes on the things above.

Yes, our body and world is fading away, but our inner man, our spirit, is being strengthened day
by day.

THE ANSWER YOU HAVE BEEN WAITING FOR

My friend, Solomon, got diagnosed with stage 4 stomach cancer out of nowhere. What they thought was just some stomach ulcers turned into a life threatening cancer. They told him he had roughly one month to live. I and some other pastors at the church came to the hospital and prayed over him, asking God to heal his body and extend his life. In the coming weeks, he started looking better and feeling healthier and not getting worse. After a few months of him doing amazingly well, they did some more tests and they couldn't find the cancer in his body like they could before.

They wouldn't name him cancer free because cancer in your stomach is incredibly hard to find on tests because of all the fluid. He just started going about his life as normal and was doing amazing. A few months later, his stomach started hurting really bad so he went in for some tests, and his colon had ripped open. It wasn't looking good. When I got to the hospital, I immediately went to debrief with his doctor to find out what was going on. The doctor told me there was nothing they could do, and he had 24-48 hours to live. I asked the doctor if he had told him and his wife yet, and he confided that he hadn't gotten the strength to do it yet.

So I went into his hospital room, looked at Solomon and his wife, Hannah, and told them the doctor said that Solomon had 24 hours to live unless God miraculously saved his life. No level of training could prepare you to have to do this. It was horrible.

After I told them the state of his situation, he stared at me for a few moments in silence. After probably 20 seconds of silence, which felt like 20 hours, he looked at me and said these words: “It's okay. I'm fine with that answer; I already made peace with Jesus about me dying.”

I was not ready for that answer. To be honest with you, I didn't like that answer. Hannah and I looked at each other and we were like, no we are going to continue praying for you! This is not the end!

He said it again “no its okay, i'm at peace”

I can't explain to you my relationship with him over the next 24 hours, getting him home, and getting him essentially prepared to die. I can't explain to you the peace he had, and I can't adequately describe to you the sense of God's nearness in that living room. It was one of the most holy and unique moments of my life. God's presence, his peace that surpasses all understanding filled the room.

Before he died, we had a party at his house. We ate, drank, laughed, worshiped and prayed. It was one of the most holy moments and tangible times with God I have had in my life.

I learned many things during those last hours, and one of the significant ones is this: you can't have the peace of God without peace with God. He had peace with God, and the peace of God filled that home.

As we come to an end of our walk together, let's dare to try to answer the question we have been wrestling with for many pages now: Why does pain happen? Why does God allow it to be a part of this human experience on this planet?

Are you ready? Here's my answer.

I don't know.

And neither do you.

And to be honest, I don't think anyone fully does. I think theologians, pastors, and counselors alike have been doing their best to answer this question from every angle we know how, but the fact is, we don't fully know. Sure, we have some good answers, we have some understanding of God and his ways. But nonetheless, it is still a mystery to us. His ways are higher than our ways and his thoughts are higher than our thoughts.

I don't fully know why God allows pain and suffering in his beautiful world, but I know that God is good. I know that He is all powerful. I know He is above my understanding and my logic. I cannot comprehend why he does certain things, and why he is absent in others. Why does he heal certain people, and not others?

But this I am certain of—God's goodness supersedes my definition of what's good. For he is justice and goodness itself.

Everyone of us reading this book right now has our own definition of what we think is good and just. If I asked 100 different people to define justice, I would get 100 different answers. The human definition of justice is a moving target.

But I deeply believe, no matter your definition of what's good, God's goodness supersedes it. He transcends our finite minds and finite perspectives.

The book of job is well known as the major book in the Bible that deals with a man's unbelievable pain and suffering. He loses everything, and I mean everything. All of his children die, he loses his health, all of his resources and finances, his entire world is burnt to the ground. Many had looked to job for the biblical answers of why does a good God allow bad things to happen.

And when you finish the book, you realize the book isn't about suffering. It's about the one who suffers. It's about the character of the man, not the state of the situation.

It's incredibly frustrating, but God doesn't answer the question. If God wanted to give us the most direct answer to the biggest question of humanity, this book was his opportunity. And he pretty much beats around the bush for 42 chapters.

But God doesn't give us an answer.

Instead he gives us Himself.

You might not like this answer, but I truly believe when it comes to pain and suffering: we don't need God's answers, we need Him.

Because even if we got the answer we were looking for, and every single detail was explained to us, it wouldn't be enough. The answer would not fix the anger, loss, pain and anguish we feel. No answer is going to fix it.

Getting the answer to the death of your child does not fix it.

Getting the answer to the loss of your spouse does not fix it.

Getting the answer to why your wife walked out on you doesn't fix it.

The answer to the pain does not fix the pain itself. It might bring momentary relief, because you can for the first time somewhat wrap your mind around the memories. But that will fade quickly, the pain will remain, and soon enough you are back to where you started.

Angry. Disillusioned. Filled with grief. Resentment welling up in your heart.

And now you have more questions. The answer to those questions now has given way to other questions. It's like a dog chasing its tail. It's not going to end. The answers are not what you need.

You see, my friend Solomon figured it out. He didn't need an answer. He needed God. He needed his presence, and for him, God's presence was enough.

You need Him. His overwhelming good, holy, and comforting presence.

Even through it all, He is worthy of worship. Through the tears he is still good. This might be the most important sentence of the whole book, please catch this.

This side of heaven is the only time I will have the chance to worship through suffering.

There is no suffering in heaven. There is no cancer, no death, no injustice.

So therefore, this is the only time you will ever have to willfully worship through the pain. And that makes your worship special.

This is the theology of pain and suffering.

Let's pray.

Father, I pray for every person finishing this book. I pray for your supernatural peace that surpasses all understanding to flood their heart. I pray for every shattered piece of their heart, and I pray you would begin to mend it, heal it, put them back together. I pray as they continue to wrestle with you, let them feel and sense your love. Let them sense your nearness. I pray in this season of their life, they would draw closer to you, more than they ever have. You are close to the broken hearted, be close to this one, too. I pray for your wisdom to fill them during this time, and help them navigate the deep waters of pain and suffering. I pray you would use this season for your glory. Let their scars be a testimony of your grace and faithfulness. I pray for those getting ready to quit and throw in the towel, give them strength and grace to go another day.

Amen.

Goodbye friends. God bless you.

Made in the USA
Columbia, SC
02 May 2025

7efa4be7-240c-400c-8001-9b5b369c7d50R02